THE CARDINAL POINTS OF BORGES

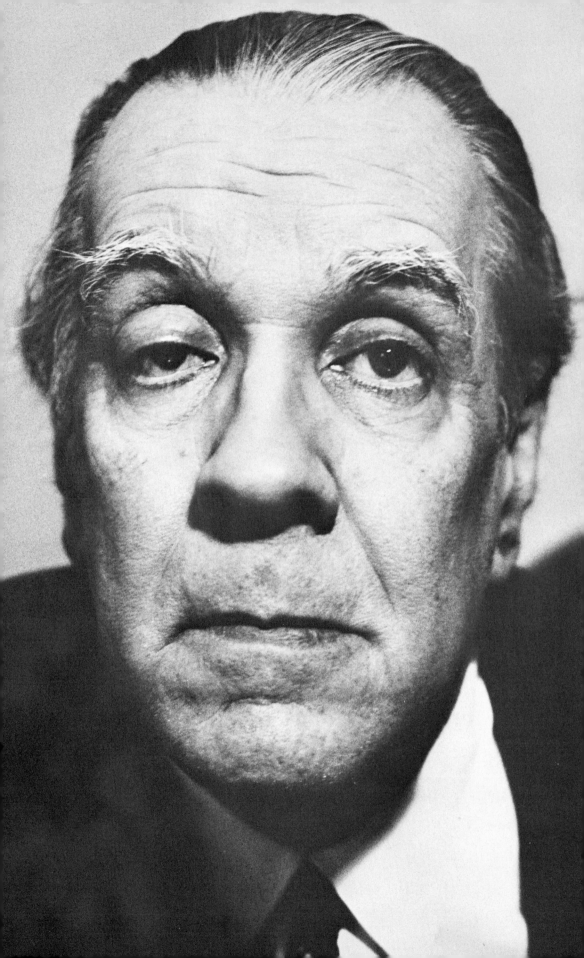

THE CARDINAL POINTS OF
Borges

Edited by LOWELL DUNHAM and IVAR IVASK

NORMAN

UNIVERSITY OF OKLAHOMA PRESS

International Standard Book Numbers:
  0–8061–0983–1 (*cloth*); 0–8061–0984–X (*paper*)

Library of Congress Catalog Card Number: 76–163635

Introduction

Julián Marías of the Spanish Royal Academy has said that Jorge Luis Borges was Jorge Luis Borges fifty years ago and just as excellent a writer then as he is today, though he had not yet begun to receive the international acclaim he now enjoys. Critics until two decades ago all but ignored Spanish America's most distinguished author. Except among a limited group of writers and readers in Spanish America, the United States, and Europe, Borges was relatively unknown and unappreciated until the 1950's, when his work was first translated into French. Since that time, Borges has become one of the most highly regarded writers of the contemporary world and the object of admiration and attention throughout the intellectual and literary circles of the last half of the twentieth century. He shared the Formentor Prize in 1960 with Samuel Beckett; he was visiting professor at the University of Texas and at Harvard, where he held the Charles Eliot Norton Chair of Poetry; he has lectured in Iowa, Michigan, Wisconsin, Utah, and other states; he was visiting professor of Spanish American Literature at the University of Oklahoma, where he also attended the second Oklahoma Conference on Writers of the Hispanic World which was dedicated to him; he has visited England, Scotland, and Israel; he was given an honorary doctorate by Oxford University; and today he is repeatedly mentioned as the outstanding candidate for the Nobel Prize for Literature.

Borges, as he prefers to be called, was born in Buenos Aires on August 24, 1899. From his father's side he comes from a long and distinguished line of military men and patriots. His maternal grandmother was English. This accounts for his lifelong interest in English and American literature and the English language. The family lived in Europe from 1914 to 1921, where Borges received much of his formal schooling. His first published work was a book of poems, *Fervor de Buenos Aires*, released in 1923. But it was in the short story that Borges early attracted attention. His two best-known short story collections, *Ficciones* (1949) and *El Aleph* (1952), he has called "my two major books."

It is perhaps in these two works that the vast knowledge and the complexity and universality of his mind are best revealed. Borges' preoccupation with encyclopedias and the man with total recall is but a reflection of the character of his own mind. It is an awe-inspiring experience to see this *monstruo de la naturaleza* in action. Few other writers of the twentieth century are his intellectual equals in the vastness and profundity of his mind. Yet it is all tempered by a modesty and gentle self-effacing humility.

Spanish American literature owes a tremendous debt to Borges. It was Borges who popularized the short story of fantasy, turning the Spanish American short story from its regionalistic, local color themes to the world of imagination. A New York critic recently credited Borges with being the most influential living writer of the contemporary short story; he has changed its theme in Western Europe and America from fact to fantasy, as he did in Spanish America. His prose style has likewise changed the prose style of most contemporary Spanish American writers; he has taught them to write in a clean, lucid, spare style that has cut away much of the pomposity and heaviness too often found in Spanish American prose.

Now almost blind, he has somehow broken the cultural barrier that makes most Spanish American, as well as Spanish, writers unknowns in the United States and much of Europe. His short stories and poetry have appeared regularly in *The New Yorker* since 1969, as well as in other literary magazines, such as *The Atlantic Monthly* and *Harpers*.

This volume is but another tribute to the man and his work. It contains the scholarly articles presented by Borges specialists at the International Symposium on Borges held at the University of Oklahoma, December 5 and 6, 1969, after his lectures on Argentine literature. Several of the contributors were among the earliest of the Borges scholars. Others were close friends who knew him and his work most intimately. The bibliographies, though not definite, as the authors point out, are a distinct contribution to Borges scholarship and will be consulted as basic bibliographical sources by all Borges scholars. The substance of this volume was first published in the Summer issue 1971 of *Books Abroad*.

Special thanks are due Thomas A. Lyon, formerly of the Department of Modern Languages, University of Oklahoma, who suggested we bring Borges to the University and who personally extended the invitation to Borges in Buenos Aires in the summer of 1969, and to other members of the working committee, James H. Abbott, Jim P. Artman, Nick Mills, and Roger Williams, all staff members of the Department of Modern Languages, University of Oklahoma, each of whom helped to make this volume possible.

Special thanks are also due to Norman Thomas di Giovanni, Borges' translator and friend, who accompanied Borges to the University of Oklahoma and who was invaluable in helping with the arrangements for both the lectures and the symposium.

Finally, special mention is made for the assistance in the preparation of this volume given by the Center for Inter-American Relations.

LOWELL DUNHAM

IVAR IVASK

Contents

Illustrations

NOTA SOBRE THE PURPLE LAND

Esta novela primigenia de Hudson es reducible a una fórmula tan antigua que
casi puede comprender la Odisea; tan elemental que sutilmente la difama y la
desvirtúa el nombre de fórmula. El héroe se echa a andar y le salen al
paso sus aventuras. A ese género nómada y azaroso pertenecen el Asno
de Oro y los fragmentos del Satiricón; Pickwick y el Don Quijote; Kim de
Lahore y Don Segundo Sombra de Areco. Llamar novelas picarescas a esas
ficciones me parece injustificado: en primer término, por la connotación
mezquina de la palabra; en segundo, por sus limitaciones locales y tem-
porales (siglo dieciséis español, siglo diecisiete). El género es complejo, por
lo demás. El desorden, la incoherencia y la variedad no son inaccesibles, pero es
indispensable que los gobierne un orden secreto, que gradualmente se descubre.
He recordado algunos ejemplos ilustres; quizá no haya uno que no exhiba
defectos evidentes. Cervantes moviliza dos tipos: un hidalgo "seco de carnes," alto,
ascético, loco y altisonante; un villano carnoso, bajo, comilón, cuerdo y ~~dicharachero.~~
esa discordia tan simétrica y persistente acaba por quitarles realidad, por
disminuirlos a figuras de circo. (En el séptimo capítulo de El Payador, nuestro
Lugones ya insinuó ese reproche.) Kipling inventa un Amiguito del Mundo Entero,
el libérrimo Kim; a los pocos capítulos, urgido por no sé qué patriótica per-
versión, le da el horrible oficio de espía. (En su autobiografía literaria, redac-

THE CARDINAL POINTS OF BORGES

JORGE LUIS BORGES

Browning resuelve ser poeta

Por estos rojos laberintos de Londres
descubro que he elegido
la más curiosa de las profesiones humanas,
salvo que todas, a su modo, lo son.
Como los alquimistas
que buscaron la piedra filosofal
en el azogue fugitivo,
haré que las comunes palabras
—naipes marcados del tahur, moneda de la plebe—
rindan la magia que fue suya
cuando Thor era el numen y el estrépito,
el trueno y la plegaria.
En el dialecto de hoy
diré a mi vez las cosas eternas;
trataré de no ser indigno
del gran eco de Byron.
Este polvo que soy será invulnerable.
Si una mujer comparte mi amor
mi verso rozará la décima esfera de los cielos concéntricos;
si una mujer desdeña mi amor
haré de mi tristeza una música,
un alto río que siga resonando en el tiempo.
Viviré de olvidarme.
Seré la cara que entreveo y que olvido,
seré Judas que acepta
la divina misión de ser un traidor,
seré Calibán en la ciénaga,
seré un soldado mercenario que muere
sin temor y sin fe,
seré Polícrates que ve con espanto
el anillo devuelto por el destino,
seré el amigo que me odia.
El persa me dará el ruiseñor y Roma la espada.
Máscaras, agonías, resurecciones
destejerán y tejerán mi suerte
y alguna vez seré Robert Browning.

Browning Decides to be a Poet

In these red labyrinths of London
I find that I have chosen
the strangest of all callings,
save that, in its way, any calling is strange.
Like the alchemists
who sought the philosopher's stone
in quicksilver,
I shall make everyday words—
the gambler's marked cards, the common coin—
give off the magic that was theirs
when Thor was both the god and the din,
the thunderclap and the prayer.
In today's dialect
I shall say, in my fashion, eternal things;
I shall try to be worthy
of the great echo of Byron.
This dust that I am will be invulnerable.
If a woman shares my love
my verse will touch the tenth sphere of the concentric heavens;
if a woman turns my love aside
I will make of my sadness a music,
a full river to resound through time.
I shall live by forgetting myself.
I shall be the face I glimpse and forget,
I shall be Judas who takes on
the divine mission of being a betrayer,
I shall be Caliban in his bog,
I shall be a mercenary who dies
without fear and without faith,
I shall be Polycrates, who looks in awe
upon the seal returned by fate.
I will be the friend who hates me.
The Persian will give me the nightingale, and Rome the sword.
Masks, agonies, resurrections
will weave and unweave my life,
and in time I shall be Robert Browning.

Translated
by
Norman Thomas di Giovanni

3

JORGE GUILLÉN

Al Margen de Borges
Encyclopaedia Britannica

Debo a la conjunción de un espejo
y de una enciclopedia el descubrimiento de Uqbar.
Ficciones, "Tlön, Uqbar, Orbis Tertius"

¡Soñemos, alma, leamos!

Entre figuras y signos
Soñemos—en la memoria—
Ajedrez, alquimia, cábala,
Palimsesto, laberinto.

Sumo jardín: biblioteca.

Escuchando, conversando
Con alfaquí, con astrólogo
Acumular un lenguaje
Donde se viva muy lejos.

¡Misteriosa Enciclopedia!

Humilde Irrealidad

Vio perros, vio un furgón en una
via muerta, vio el horizonte, vio un
caballo plateado que bebía el
agua crapulosa de un charco.

"La muerte y la brújula"

I

Vi la tierra de nadie, ni suburbio
Ni campina en un gris ocaso turbio.
Sin sentir la atracción del horizonte,
Vi un perro que husmeaba en un desmonte
El postrer comestible desperdicio.
Vi una herrumbrosa via sin servicio.
Vi un famélico gato que bebía
Los reflejos del sol y su agonía
Sobre un agua de lluvia ahora charco.

Todo estaba en un óleo sin marco.

II

Yo no sé si en pintura acierto o fallo.
El óleo compré.
                    Con un caballo
Soñé que de aquel lienzo sin motivo
Surgía, solitario como chivo,
También remoto si se ve de cerca.
Más: soñé con el agua de un alberca.
Ya la errante figura allí se inclina
Para saciar su triste sed equina.

Ay, se me fue del lienzo aquel caballo.
Con palabras lo busco y sí lo hallo.

Este en bruma vidente
Que discurre, distante, melancólico,
Proponiendo vocablos
De luz desde la sombra,
Este moderno austral
Con tan nuevas penumbras milenarias:
Hacedor y dicente.

A Modest Proposal
for the Criticism of Borges

By RONALD CHRIST

I.

Borges' writing is instinct with its own criticism—with both the method and matter of that criticism. Critics have, therefore, imitated him in writing about him: he searches sources, and so do they; he pretends to believe in the trivial meaninglessness of individual personality, and so do they; he reiterates from story to poem to essay identical themes of time and literature, often in the same language, and so do they—repeating each other—from review to article to book. (A conspiratorial theory of Borges criticism is bound to occur to anyone reading much of it, not to speak of someone writing any of it. The reason for dismissing the suspicion, however, is obvious: it is too *Tlön*, too perfectly Borgesean.) But the most startling of Borges' devices has not yet, as far as I know, found its way into the writings about him, even though it is no less legitimate or illuminating than the appropriation of his own vocabulary to describe him, a practice almost all his critics pursue. The device I have in mind is the one of presenting brief projections or synopses (or even evaluations, since critical writings are criticized too) of imagined but not yet written critical and interpretative works as if those works had already undergone the tedious processes of development, elaboration, and extensive documentation, not to mention stylistic refinement.

In his prologue to the collection of stories entitled "The Garden of the Forking Paths," which appeared in 1941, Borges wrote:

> A laborious and impoverishing extravagance—that is what the composition of long books is: the expansion to five hundred pages of an idea whose perfect oral exposition takes a few minutes. A better procedure is to imagine that these books already exist and to offer a résumé, a commentary. That is what Carlyle did in *Sartor Resartus* and Butler in *The Fair Haven*—works which have the imperfection of being books, too, no less tautological than others. More reasonable, more inept, more indolent, I have preferred writing notes about imaginary books. These are "Tlön, Uqbar, Orbis Tertius," the "Examination of the Works of Herbert Quain," "The Approach to Al-Mu'tasim."

I see no reason why the same principle should not be applied to the criticism of Borges. None of us is ashamed to admit that he has learned or reapprehended a cyclical theory of time from Borges, a theory which we then apply to Borges' own works as well as

7

to the works of other writers. None of us would be embarrassed to read or undertake a study of Borges which established the two or three fundamental metaphors in his work, basing ourselves all the while on the tentative dictum in his essay "Pascal's Sphere": "Perhaps universal history is the history of a few metaphors." We are not embarrassed in these instances, I believe, because we are dealing with the ideas or "content" of the man's work; and school as well as books about books have taught us that content is available for discussion—desirous, even, of reproduction. Hence we have the history of ideas, a discipline into which many of Borges' writings fit. (I am thinking of essays like "Pascal's Sphere," which I just mentioned, or "The History of Eternity.") Yet once we move away from the man's ideas and intuitions, from the intellectual and emotional content of the man's art, shame overcomes us. We are numb to the possibilities of his form. Unafraid to use anything he may imagine against him, we are still afraid to turn his own form on him. We hesitate to manipulate the models of brevity and résumé—coupled with comment, which he demonstrates and recommends, at the same time that we busy ourselves tracking down the influences and sources—which he also recommends. This lopsided attention to the imaginative possibilities in Borges' work prevents us from valuing one of the chief gifts of his art: the rehabilitation of the critical act as an agent of swift insight, pleasurable contemplation and, possibly, lasting reverberation.

Of course I am not encouraging either rigid imitation of Borges or vulgar parody; all I am urging is that we take advantage of an opportunity discovered for us by Borges himself. In stories like "Examination of the Works of Herbert Quain" Borges taught us that criticism is in no way inferior to art but simply that critics have been inferior to artists; he has restored to us the knowledge that the achievements of literary criticism are subordinate to those of fiction and poetry, necessarily, only when the motives are different. In other ages, Horace and Pope have known that; in our time, along with Borges, the author of a volume of notes to his own translation of *Eugene Onegin* has also known it. We certainly cannot equal these achievements, but even reconciling ourselves to a second order of criticism, we can learn from them. So what I am urging is the adoption of Borges' innovation as a means of criticism—that innovation he first tried in 1935 with "The Approach to Al-Mu'tasim," epitomized in "Pierre Menard, Author of *Quixote*" and perfected in "Tlön, Uqbar, Orbis Tertius."

If we follow Borges' lead, modifying it for our purposes, the results will be, I think, substantial. First of all, more criticism—more essential and exciting criticism at that—will be written; second, *much* more criticism will be read; and third, but most important, the effect of criticism on the reader will be enhanced. Instead of passively following an article or book from its two-part title (a title separated from its subtitle by a dash or colon, depending on how pretentious the ensuing argument will be) to its abundantly proven conclusion, the reader's mind will actively stir with thoughts and imaginings and discoveries all its own. In this respect, criticism will in some small way capture an effect of Borges' fiction, which agitates more by concrete suggestion and implication than it does by lavishness of evidence or processes of solution: witness the bibliography of Pierre Menard's works and the cataloguing of Orbis Tertius' qualities, which aesthetically hint at much more than they actually exhibit.

In his essay "The Wall and the Books," Borges has tentatively defined the aesthetic events as the "imminence of a revelation which is not produced," a definition he echoes at the conclusion of his recent narrative "Pedro Salvadores," where he says, in Norman Thomas di Giovanni's translation, that Salvadores "strikes us as a symbol of something we are about to understand, but never quite do." And surely much of the genuinely psychosomatic sensation engendered by his writing comes from the glimpsed contact with such an imminence. Why not, then, imbue criticism with a similar imminence whose revelation will take place, if at all, in the mind of the reader, where it should have the most meaningful expression and the most lasting importance anyway? In this manner criticism could participate, if not in the aesthetic event Borges describes, at least in an imaginative one.

II.

The following eight items are, then, summaries or projections of works about Borges which have been conceived by their wholly imaginary authors but never written; they are offered as possible samples of the criticism I have adumbrated. Whether they are summaries of the fictitious notes, the mythical essays or of the hypothetical monographs I have labored *not* to write is wholly dependent on the degree of reverberation they create in the reader, whose mind is the pages on which they are written and whose thought is the vocabulary in which they are finally expressed.

The Verbal Poverty of Jorge Luis Borges

Noting that Ana María Barrenechea has compiled a huge and nearly exhaustive concordance of Borges' most expressive words, this projector proposes a more difficult task for himself. He has decided to refine that concordance of words which Borges repeats with mannered frequency in agreement with a statement Borges made in an early essay called "A Profession of Literary Faith": "I have already overcome my poverty; I have recognized, among thousands, the nine or ten words which accord with my heart . . . ." If the reader can recognize those words, the author argues, then the reader will have no less surely recognized the heart of Borges.

After establishing his list of words (among them "annihilate," "arduous," "decipher," and "verisimilar") the author demonstrates that these words reflect in their repeated frequency and peculiar usage ("the arduous pupils of Pythagoras" in the poem "The Cyclical Night" for example) a hard-won, personal idiom, no less intimate in fact and no less impersonal in appearance than the repetitive red, blue, and yellow squares of Mondrian.

The author concludes by refusing to see his list of key words as final and suggests the possibility of other, equally valid lists: the most obvious one is a time-space list; another would be a list for the young Borges, emphasizing words like *ocaso, calle, arrabal*; more provocative is one he calls "The Idiom of Abomination," headed by the ubiquitous "atrocious." Finally, the author suggests that in place of writing more interpretations of Borges' works, each critic restrict himself to drawing up a list of the nine or ten words which constitute, in his opinion, the words with which Borges conquered his poverty.

The Metaphorical Borges

In general, critics have agreed that after his first collections of essays Borges forsook the elaborately metaphorical style which characterized his earliest prose and was the foundation of his early poetry. They agree, moreover, that his mature fiction is virtually devoid of metaphor. A detailed analysis of Borges' stories, however, shows that many metaphors are imbedded in the prose texture and suggests that translators and critics alike, by virtue of not believing in their existence, have failed to see them.

Furthermore, as the imaginary being who is the author of this non-existent argument explains, Borges' prose is not only richly, though elusively, metaphorical; these metaphors are neither decorative nor merely evocative, but rather "architectural," serving to mark important shifts in character and plot. Among the examples he cites is one from "The Circular Ruins," where the outcome of the story involves a shattering of the priest's sense of reality when he discovers that he too, like the son he has dreamed, is a creation of fire. This ending is a surprise, and one of the most moving scenes in Borges' fiction; but, as this analysis points out, Borges has been careful to predict, by means of a cunning metaphor, the real, fiery, nature of the priest's world long before the end of the story.

You will remember that as the priest introduces the dreamed boy into the real world the text reads: "Gradually he was accustoming him to reality. Once he ordered him to place a flag on a distant peak. The next day the flag was flapping on the peak." In Spanish, the word which is translated here as "flapping" and elsewhere, with more accuracy, as "fluttering" is *flameaba*, which can mean "fluttering" or "billowing" like a sail, but can also mean "emitting flames." That the story enforces this last sense is confirmed by the conclusion, where Borges writes that the priest walked into the *jirones de fuego*, a phrase meaning "tatters of flame" but one which can also mean "banners" or "pennants of flame." The metaphor *jirones de fuego* echoes the flag which flamed from the peak: on the one hand the flag flames; on the other the flames flag, which is to say that flag and flames are identical, and the priest's proof of the boy's having entered the real world, the fluttering flag, is as incorporeal or fiery as everything else in the story.

Thus this study opens the way to an entirely new notion of the use of metaphor in Borges, and, probably, to a whole series of doctoral dissertations as well.

Borges and Kafka: Dark Laughter in the Parables

After enumerating all the obvious and belabored similarities between the short fiction of Borges and Kafka, this visionary study dismisses these resemblances as trivial and fortuitous, stressing in their place the one thing these two writers really have in common: a prankish sense of humor yoked to bureaucratic gloom on the one hand and to metaphysical melancholy on the other but in both cases asserting itself ultimately as "cosmic comedy." Unfortunately for his argument, however, the author is unable to establish that Borges, as is well known of Kafka, giggled to himself as he composed his stories.

A Special Problem in the Translation of Borges

To translate Borges is to encounter the phenomenon and problem of his Latinity. His writing is Latinate in a peculiar way, and this translator pleads for a reexamination of these Latinisms.

First of all, the translator argues, we must discount certain of Borges' statements about his writing. Citing an interview, the translator quotes Borges to the effect that there are too many Latin words in the translation of his works:

> A good translation, no? Except that there are too many Latin words in it. For example, if I wrote, just say, *habitación oscura* (I wouldn't, of course, have written *that*, but *cuarto oscuro*, but just say I did), then the temptation is to translate *habitación* with *habitation*, a word which sounds close to the original. But the word I want is *room*: it is more definite, simpler, better.

Juxtaposed to this passage, the translator quotes two sentences from *Ficciones*, one from "Death and the Compass" and the other from "The South," which use the word *habitación* in exactly the way Borges rejects. Then, with evident pleasure, he quotes a passage from "The Intruder"—Borges' most manneristically simple story and one which was written not long before the interview quoted above took place—and in the passage still another example of *habitación* occurs! Thus, the translator deduces, if oblique Latinisms abound in the English versions of Borges, there is elaborate cause in the Spanish originals.

Then this projector goes on to show that Borges, ever since praising Sir Thomas Browne's "imperial Latinity" in an essay first published in 1925, has himself relied heavily on Latinisms with a special intention and an unusual practice. The intention is the one ascribed to Brown: "the earnest desire for universality and clarity," while the unusual practice consists in frequently using the Latin derivative not in its commonly accepted sense submerged in Spanish use, but in an English manner. That is to say, a rarer meaning. A problematic example, meaningful chiefly because it recurs so frequently in Borges, is the word *notorio* which in Spanish usually retains the Latin sense of *notus*, meaning well known or obvious. Borges, the translator argues, almost always uses this word with its more typically English significance of known unfavorably or infamous. A sentence like the one which opens the story "Theme of the Traitor and the Hero" must therefore be translated "Under the notorious influence of Chesterton." A conclusive example occurs in "Death and the Compass." Borges is describing the Hôtel du Nord, where the first murder takes place. He writes: "this tower (which *notoriamente* unites the hateful whiteness of a sanitorium, the numbered divisibility

11

of a prison and the general appearance of a brothel) . . . ." It seems clear from the context of "hateful," "prison," and "brothel" that *notoriamente* here must be translated in the English sense of "notoriously," not "manifestly" as one translator has it or even "glaringly" as another renders it. This revision merits attention, because it shows how Borges is able to make a relatively inert word serve the purpose of his world-view by including it in what has elsewhere been described as his "Idiom of Abomination."

The translator ends by observing that Borges' international success is a product of his quest for universality, which has led him to compose in several languages simultaneously: he writes in Spanish with Latin words and achieves English meaning.

A Counterfactual History of Literature

As this fanciful writer explains in his preface, counterfactual history or counterfactual economics is history or economics which "involves a comparison between what actually happened and what would have happened in the absence of a specified circumstance." For example, R. W. Fogel, in an article which appeared in the *Economic Review*, recommends a recounting of the way the United States would have been settled if the railroads had not existed.* Of course this is an exceedingly difficult task, for Fogel himself remarks that "since the counterfactual condition never occurred, it could not have been observed and hence is not recorded in historical documents." Nevertheless, our projector, an undaunted admirer of counterfact, has applied the theory to literature and with a wealth of anti-evidence at his disposal has come up with the first counterfactual history of literature.

In an early chapter he describes the evolution of Greek drama without Aeschylus' introduction of the second actor; in another chapter he examines the way in which Chaucer composed "The Romance of the Rose" without the French original; and in the last chapter he analyzes how Borges wrote "Borges y Yo" without one of the Borgeses ever having existed.

This study is not as valuable for what it provides as it is for what it predicts: not only will we someday have "The Development of the United States without Railroads," but we will also be able to read "A History of English Literature without Shakespeare" and "A History of Argentine Literature without Borges." Forgetting will be history's way of remembering; the eternal monument will be a willed oblivion.

Almost needless to say, this projector modestly fails to imagine a history of criticism without him.

The World of Borges

"To add provinces to Being, to hallucinate cities and spaces," wrote Borges, "is an heroic adventure"; but few critics have emphasized the phenomenology of his world. This projected study does that, showing how Borges' fiction defines an abstract,

*R. W. Fogel, "The New Economic History, Its Findings and Methods," *Economic Review*, Second Series, vol. 19.

mythologized world which is neither Buenos Aires, India, nor the setting of any of his stories, but a general, universalized space in which six spatial phenomena govern and recur like the suits in a Tarot deck: the window or doorway, the garden, the tower, the cellar, the staircase, and the wall or corridor. Within the context of these spaces other phenomena—the knife, the mirror, the book—operate. Action in this world is formalized into vertical and horizontal movement, and the fundamental ritual, according to the projector of this study, is "The Rite of the Knife," frequently enacted as "The Ceremony of the Labyrinth."

Despite the prejudicial fashionability of phenomenological studies, this one is solid. It is based on the facts of Borges' stories and corresponds minutely to the system of his thought. The final sentence of the essay—"In Borges' world the metaphysic predicts the iconography"—seems incontrovertible.

Borges' Prose: A Question of Genre

Discounting the classifications of novel, romance, and autobiography, this projector, a disciple of Northrop Frye, categorizes Borges' prose as Menippean satire or anatomy. His argument is based on Frye's description of Menippean satire in the essay "Four Types of Prose Fiction"; and the key quotations from Frye are two: first, "The Menippean satire deals less with people as such than with mental attitudes"; and, second, "The Menippean satirist, dealing with intellectual themes and attitudes, shows his exuberance in intellectual ways, by piling up an enormous mass of erudition about his theme." The association between other Menippean satirists—Burton, Swift, Voltaire, Huxley—and Borges does more for an understanding of the simultaneous originality and traditionality of Borges' prose fictions than do any of the previously suggested generic labels like *conte philosophique* or the even vaguer "metaphysical fiction."

Lamentably pedantic, this study is worthwhile chiefly for its culmination in an extended comparison between some of the most characteristically Borgesean stories and Pope's *Variorum*, which leads the author to emphasize three of Borges' most neglected qualities: his comedy, his satire, his neoclassicism.

Borges: Monstrorum Artifex

> Chesterton, it seems to me, would not have tolerated the imputation of being a weaver of nightmares, a *monstrorum artifex* (Pliny, XXVIII, 12), but, invincibly, he tends to lapse into atrocious observations.

From early works like the "History of Angels," which appeared in 1926, to late ones like *The Book of Imaginary Beings*, which was published in 1967, Borges has always been interested in monsters and the monstrous. This projection asserts that the idea of the monster is at the core of Borges' fictional world, yielding not only his most important symbol, but also the form of some of his most outstanding fiction, and, in part, the content as well.

The labyrinth, of course, is the symbol; and a quotation from *The Book of Imaginary Beings* supports the assertion:

> The idea of a house built so that people lose themselves in it is perhaps stranger than the idea of a man with the head of a bull, but the two assist each other and the image of the labyrinth corresponds to the image of the minotaur. It is fitting that there be a monstrous inhabitant at the center of a monstrous house.

Hence a story like "The House of Asterion"; hence the two overlapping bestiaries: "The Manual of Fantastic Zoology" and *The Book of Imaginary Beings*.

More ingenious, though, is the way this chain of reasoning shows Borges' love of the monstrous in the ideas he cultivates. Simply stated, the argument is that Borges seeks intellectual aberrations and monsters or, to use Borges' own word for them, "heresys." (Heresy is the intellectual equivalent of physical monstrosity, and even Borges' denial of time is a monstrous heresy in which Borges himself admittedly has no faith.) With great diligence, the pervasive presence of real or imagined heresies and heresiarchs are pointed out in the Borges canon. The story "The Theologians" is one clear case in point; "Tlön, Uqbar, Orbis Tertius" is another, subtler one: much of the information we have about Tlön is attributed to heresiarchs by the apocryphal encyclopedia.

Less tenable, but more stimulating is the declaration that the essay-story form of works like "The Approach to Al-Mu'tasim" is attributable to Borges' creation of monsters. Borges' definition of a monster is quoted from "Fantastic Zoology": "a monster is nothing else but a combination of elements from real beings" and thus, it is reasoned, as an angel is a monster composed of a man's body and a bird's wings, "The Approach to Al-Mu'tasim" is a monster composed of an essay's form and a story's content.

The manifest advantage of this explanation of Borges' art is its cohesiveness: its ability to align disparate works, to put poems like "The Golem" in meaningful relation to essays like "A New Refutation of Time"; but the real value lies in its pointing to a special pleasure provided by Borges: the startling satisfaction derived from the exhibition of mental monsters. Borges himself, it is noted, has wondered if his most famous fictions are not "freaks," and with proper humility the projector ends by asking if Borges' works are simply a sideshow in the circus of literature.

III.

What I have written is now, already, receding in your memory—that medium of refinement and loss which Borges has written of with such feeling—and what I have tried to suggest in the preceding projections is the possibility of writing directly for that medium rather than for intervening states of awareness. In such criticism, the attempt is to make you feel that you have already experienced the full argument and are now reviewing its essence, either extending its import with the stock of your perceptions and recollections or rejecting it with the weight of your knowledge and information—or lack of interest. In either case, the emphasis is on you as agent and the original work as object, and the criticism is a stripped, intermediary invention whose aim is not the presentation of disclosures but the possible production of them in you. Admittedly, the examples I have given are questionable, but perhaps they can provoke better ones.

So, at last, I come to my proposal, which, swiftly formulated, is that we found a publication in honor of Borges—a journal or newsletter that will embody the kind of criticism I have dimly suggested. A new criticism of ingenuity and provocation, one that is prodigal with ideas and miserly with self-expression; a new publication devoted to the résumé of thoughts joined to brief commentary, preferably antagonistic, on those thoughts; a new publication whose yearly issues will fill only a page or two but whose lines will speak volumes. Truly a little magazine, one whose articles will not permit time or space for the flash of expectation aroused by their titles to dissipate in wearisome exegesis or repetitive development.

The soundness of my proposal can be easily tested: ask yourself what you remember from the last articles and books you read, beyond their titles and, perhaps, an idea or two—that, and a sense of time spent in reading. I contemplate a publication which would present *only* those titles and ideas; perhaps, in the best of cases, simply a table of contents and an annual bibliography. The duration of criticism will be nobly sacrificed to its essence. The practice of my proposal is already being tested by the Modern Language Association, which has begun, surreptitiously, to precede its articles with brief abstracts, with the result that readers of the abstracts cannot be distinguished from readers of the articles. (Of course it should be noted that Borges was an honorary member of that organization for several years before the practice was actually started.) The efficacy of my proposal is self-evident: criticism will attain the impact of a drawing whose whole pattern and form are seized in a moment.

Borges has foreseen the end of the lengthy novel and the survival of the short story; let us foresee the end of typical criticism and the endurance of the stimulating remark, the impelling or even exasperating insight. As a first step toward the realization of this goal, I reject the excessiveness of all that I have written and offer in its place a self-sufficient title: "Pierre Menard, Critic of Borges."   *Rutgers University*

In the Labyrinth

By EMIR RODRÍGUEZ MONEGAL

> this city which I believed was my past
> is my future, my present;
> the years I've lived in Europe are a delusion,
> I have always been (and always will be) in Buenos Aires.
>
> *Obra poética* (1964)*

There is a Buenos Aires which everyone can see. The modern city which grows in leaps and bounds imitating Chicago or New York, after having imitated Paris and London, and even before, those modest Spanish or Italian prototypes dreamt up by the immigrants. It is an infernal city in the summer (in this also it imitates New York), and it is damp and frigid in winter. It is also a great city, the greatest concentration of people in the Hispanic world. It is majestic and pathetic, ignoble and proud, a human labyrinth like so many others. There, close to one of the busiest streets, Florida, and on the edge of one of the principal parks, San Martín, lives a man for whom Buenos Aires is a totally different city, or several different ones, none of which coincides with the gray, real one. That man, Borges, is almost blind but until recently he used to go out on the street alone. He would take as his only guide and support a white cane and the inner knowledge of a city which he has made his by recreating it as myth. It was quite easy to find him on Florida, elbowing his way through the invisible crowd with that absent and at the same time concentrated manner of a man who has other means of vision than most people. His face seemed fixed, unexpressive until you saw his eyes, completely turned inward in a permanent expression of painful surprise. Borges could walk around Buenos Aires, navigate through its crowds, lose himself in its labyrinth because his eyes are open to a reality all his own, not less but more real than the other one.

The Buenos Aires which he is still seeing disappeared many years ago, at the turn of the century, but Borges has not lost the gift of recreating it with his words. Chance has afforded me many opportunities to walk the streets of Buenos Aires with Borges during the space of two decades. Each one of these experiences had a disquieting effect on me. Because I (who see merely with the eyes of the flesh) was constantly compelled

---

*This quote is from "Arrabal," considerably altered in 1964 from the 1921 edition of *Obra poética* (Buenos Aires, Emecé Editores). The verses summarize Borges' present vision of Buenos Aires. The original lines are:

> esta ciudad que yo creí mi pasado
> es mi porvenir, mi presente;
> los años que he vivido en Europa son ilusorios,
> yo he estado siempre (y estaré) en Buenos Aires.

by Borges to see what was no longer there and, nevertheless, was more there than the chaotic, rapidly vanishing surface that my eyes could see. Borges' words, his deep and warm intonation, momentarily created for me a Buenos Aires which time has destroyed. It is about the Buenos Aires I had the privilege of glimpsing through his words and gestures that I would like to write now.

I first went to Buenos Aires in 1946 during the Perón regime. I had met Borges the previous year in Montevideo, where I lived. In those times, Montevideo seemed friendlier to him than Buenos Aires, and he used to cross the River Plate to lecture and to visit relatives and friends. We tried to repay his visits as often as we could. Buenos Aires was then literally wall-papered with enormous posters of Perón and his blond companion, covered with generally aggressive slogans. The city had the look of an occupied town, marked here and there with great empty lots—that of the Jockey Club, right on Florida, which had witnessed one of the fires fomented if not actually set by the regime against the landowner's oligarchy—it was a city which grew sad with the furtive looks many of the proud Argentines now wore. In that insulted Buenos Aires, Borges walked anxiously. He was in his late forties and, although nearsighted, could see better then. He didn't use a cane, and his step was more nervous, almost brusque. Only when crossing the streets would a natural prudence make him hold his companion by the sleeve, rather than the arm, with an imperious gesture which requested but did not beg help. With the same sudden brusqueness he'd let go on the other side. But verbal communication never stopped.

Borges dimly saw (or guessed) the slogans of the regime, the infinite repetition of Perón's and Evita's names, the calculated humiliation of patrician Buenos Aires. But he couldn't keep quiet about it. He'd point to each enormous letter, underline each slogan, talk and talk furiously. The Buenos Aires of his poems and dreams, the suburban quarters with its general stores and pink corners and its local gangsters covered with white soft hats, its twilights and streets more and more open to the invading pampas, was gone. Nothing was left of that mythical Buenos Aires of his tales. Now the city was covered by the posters of a regime which took on the moral task of breaking the back of a powerful oligarchy which had dreamt in cement of London and Paris. Borges was not excessively pained by the humiliation of a class whose pretentious weaknesses he had always satirized, but by the demagoguery of this *jefe* who aired social grudges, petty fascist lessons, in a colossal display of mediocrity. While he walked, Borges could not stop talking. His pain was visible in the bitterness of his intonation, in his brusque gestures, more than in the actual words. He was like a man skinned alive. Here and there, the real Buenos Aires was visible to him. But from his talk a different, more ominous city emerged. It was a city of unrelieved horror, the one that is transcribed phantasmagorically and under European names in "The Death and the Compass." Only a thin disguise of chess board geometry and Chestertonian paradox separated that city where Good and Evil fought from the real one. The same gray nightmarish Buenos Aires reappears in "The Wait," where a man waits for his enemies to kill him. It also is the sordid background of "The Monster's Celebration," a parodic transcription of one of Perón's big rallies, written in collaboration with Bioy Casares. The ugliness of the Perón capital is at the back of some of the more dismal tales of this period.

Listening to Borges, it was impossible not to feel a kind of rejection mixed with a quiet impatience. I was not afraid that somebody could hear us. The regime was too disorganized and chaotic to provide that type of menace. It is true that it set out to persecute the intellectuals, but it did it in a casual inconsistent manner. For having signed a democratic manifesto, Borges was demoted from a humble position in a suburban library to the inspection of fowls in a municipal market. To his lectures, no matter how esoteric the subject, the police always sent one man to take notes and report immediately. His mother and his sister were sentenced to prison for one month for having dared to sing the national anthem in a demonstration on Florida. His sister went to prison (with another distinguished friend, Victoria Ocampo) and his mother was kept under vigilance in her own apartment. These petty persecutions were designed more to humiliate than to frighten.

I knew all this, and that is why my rejection came not because his words seemed wrong to me; it was for something else. I felt the shame of a person who spies on someone elses nightmare, who involuntarily listens to the cries and private words of a sleeper. Brutally, the passion with which Borges denounced Perón's Buenos Aires brought me into his own labyrinth. Listening to him, sympathizing with him, I wanted nevertheless to say "No," to argue that Perón was more than a mediocre tyrant, that he meant something completely different for the workers and the poor people, that he had introduced new and just laws, that he was trying (perhaps unsuccessfully) to liberate Argentina from the foreign powers. I wanted to tell him that the sinister Buenos Aires of his tales and nightmares hardly existed in reality, or had another more bureaucratic mask of informers, petty dealers, and arbitrary policemen. But how can one establish a dialogue with a dreamer? Borges imposed his nightmare upon me and I ended up by feeling the viscosity of the air, the menace of the walls, the obsessive presence of the names repeated by every slogan. His vision had created a labyrinth in this mediocre reality and I also was lost in it.

As soon as we reached the South Side of Buenos Aires, Borges' mood would change. The South Side seems (or seemed in those years of 1946 to 1949, which I am now evoking) like the setting of a Borges tale. He would drag me to see some surviving pink corner; we would step into patios which still had the stone pavement of another tyrant's times: this Juan Manuel de Rosas who comes obsessively into his verses; we would cross squares still damp with the dampness that chilled his grandparents. Sometimes, in the evening, we would land in some café where a little band continued to play the tangos of the Old Guard while at the back you could hear the incessant, ghostly, clacking of billiard balls. Then, for a minute, Borges would forget Perón and would even laugh. He would tap the table with his hand (somewhat short, with fat fingers) to the rhythms of an old tango. I used to think then that Borges was providing me with local color, that he wanted to show the tourist (a Uruguayan is always a bit provincial in Buenos Aires) the remains, or perhaps the debris, of a mythical Buenos Aires which still lives in his poems and in his biography of the suburban poet, Evaristo Carriego. But there was something more than that in his mind. Through that tango ritual, Borges managed to escape for a moment from Perón's moral prison, from the loud walls of his own nightmare. The Buenos Aires he loved was still alive in the music of the tango.

We often walked the streets of the South Side and also some quarters of the poorer North Side which has nothing to do with the brilliant one of the *señoritos* and the fashionable stores of Florida. I still remember one night when we walked through half of Buenos Aires (he was a great walker then and enjoyed the quietness of suburban nights) to see a friend who lived in a Jewish neighborhood of sad and dusty trees. On that occasion Perón was dropped from the conversation, which branched off into the labyrinths of English literature which Borges knows and loves so much. Stevenson, Chesterton, Kipling, James filled the solitary streets with their inventions, brought to life by Borges' precise words. "Don't you agree?" he never tired of asking me with the most flawless courtesy. Quoting texts and commenting on them, developing hints and pursuing allusions, Borges had managed to create, on the border of the Peronist madness, an entire world and had succeeded again in dragging me into the labyrinth of books.

For a while, I decided not to go back to Buenos Aires. Perón was making things very difficult for the Uruguayans and what was to be called the Tin Curtain had already begun to alienate those two countries, more united than separated by the River Plate. Borges kept coming to Montevideo, to lecture and to be feted by us. But even his visits became scarce toward the end of the regime. Only some years later, in 1956, when a military revolution returned Argentina to the army and cattle oligarchy which had always governed it, I crossed the river again and met Borges in his own country. He was euphoric at that time. He would endlessly repeat his loyalty to the new regime that repaired Perón's persecution by naming him Director of the National Library. Borges could again breathe in a city now freed of certain demons. Once again we took a walk through the South Side. We went into a Greek church in which the still air seemed solid and the light was barely more than a dusky shade. The pale gold ornaments were alive in an atmosphere completely void of human presence. In that expressionistic setting which looks out of some of his minutely precise stories, Borges seemed to be in his natural habitat. The darkness of the church was his light.

He took me out to dinner, with some mutual friends, at an old warehouse of the Rosas era. The entranceway was through one of the carriage porches which appear in some of his poems. The somber stone-paved patio, the moist plants branching off against the walls of dirty whitewash, an old mail coach which perhaps carried Facundo Quiroga to his death in Barranca Yaco (as Borges' famous poem tells), were the portico of an enormous room of thin wooden columns which suggested a stable rather than a restaurant. There we talked again about literature, contemporary and old. But Borges was more interested in something else. He never tired of making me see, of looking through my eyes, at that relic of Rosas' time. In his personal memory, the retrospective hate against the old tyrant, inherited from grandfathers and great-grandfathers, now blended almost perfectly with the hate for Perón. It was easy to see that Perón and

Rosas were now one, and both served as a metaphor for Borges' attraction toward these cynical men, with their jagged knives or electric shock treatment, those smiling traitors of Argentine history he despises but cannot help but admire. This writer, obsessed by the consciousness of not having lived enough, saw in these men of action the exact counterpart of his own meditative self: he was the man of books, they were the men with knives. He denounced them in poems and stories, and, at the same time, they held a horrible fascination for him. They were the "other," the dark side of the self. Now that Perón was gone, Borges could go back to Rosas.

The reality of Borges, of the concrete person who is Borges, hit me again one day when he invited me to tour the National Library. The building over which Paul Groussac had presided was already going to seed but still had a certain grandeur. Built for the National Lottery, it was destined to house the National Library: a fact that symbolically anticipated two of Borges' most celebrated stories: "The Lottery of Babylon" and "The Library of Babel." But at the time I didn't know this and entered the Library without any allegorical qualms. Borges took me in hand and moved around without seeing much but seeing enough to know where each book he wanted was. He can open a book to the desired page and without bothering to read—through an effort of memory parallel only to those of his Irinero Funes—quote complete pages. He roams along corridors lined with books, he quickly turns corners and gets into passages which are truly invisible, mere cracks in the walls of books, he rushes down winding staircases which abruptly end in the dark. There is almost no light in these corridors and staircases. I try to follow him, tripping, blinder and more handicapped than Borges because my only guides are my eyes. In the dark of the library Borges finds his way with the precarious precision of a tightrope-walker. Finally, I come to understand that the space in which we are momentarily inserted is not real: it is a space made of words, signs, symbols. It is another labyrinth. Borges drags me in, makes me quickly descend the long winding staircase, fall exhausted into the center of darkness. Suddenly, there is light at the end of another corridor. Prosaic reality awaits me there. Next to Borges who smiles like a child who has played a joke on a friend, I recover my eyesight, the real world of light and shadow, the conventions I am trained to recognize. But I come out of the experience like one who emerges from the deep of water or of dream, shattered by the (other) reality of that labyrinth of paper.

When I saw Borges again in the summer of 1962, in Buenos Aires, the city was already different. He had just returned from the States and Europe, and the "fathers of the country" were again mobilizing their troops to save the democracy in danger. The recent elections which gave to the Peronist the victory in a good part of Argentina, were being voided by the army. The President, a talented and ineffectual civilian, gave in to military pressure. Buenos Aires had again taken on the ominous look of a city occupied by its own army. I hadn't seen Borges for some years (five, at least) and I found him very changed. All the newspapers were saying he was totally blind but I saw him coming alone, with his cane and luminous gaze, swiftly cutting through the human traffic of Florida. We had an appointment in front of a well-known café, The Richmond, and went to have lunch in a nearby Italian restaurant. My eagerness to hear all about him hurried the conversation a bit, I fear. He looked subtly dilapidated by time: his hair grayer, his cheeks more flaccid, his movements less sure. He told me that they greatly exaggerated his blindness, that newspapermen had transformed him into a pathetic figure because a nearsighted man sells less copy than a blind one. (Oedipus in Buenos Aires, I didn't dare to say.) In the States he had seen the movie version of *The Turn of the Screw*, one of his favorite novels, and he was enthusiastic about it. I knew that movies were one of his old passions. Having seen some films with him, I also knew that he doesn't need much to be able to follow a film. I figured that the contrasted images of the big screen were perhaps clearer to him than bungling reality, carelessly edited and illuminated, much less neat.

Although Borges spoke with enthusiasm about many things, he seemed sad. He could not avoid mentioning the illegality of what was then happening in Argentina. Although he still was anti-Peronist (he still is), he could not fail to say that if the Peronist had been voted for, the results of the election had to be accepted. For once, I agreed with him on a political matter. As I was leaving for the States in a few days, we exchanged some rapid impressions of a country which Borges had just visited for the first time and which was beginning to discover him. He was fascinated with the American experience. I suspected that in the States, Borges had collected images that were based more on the books he had read and reread—those of Poe, Hawthorne and Emerson, Whitman and Mark Twain, James and William Faulkner—than those based on a reality which was already beginning to become completely invisible.

With mock eloquence, he tried to convince me to give up all projects (including a biography of him) and dedicate myself exclusively to the study of Anglo-Saxon literature. He recited obscure fragments in a tongue I hardly recognized because although it is the ancestor of English it is separated from it by all that English has of French, Latin, and Mediterranean. The archaic verses sounded like a prayer, or an exorcism, in the mouth of Borges who doubtlessly added unpredictable River Plate inflections. With the solemnity with which one should answer a joke, I told him that it was impossible for me to follow him into the labyrinth of that early literature. He didn't seem to regret it. I now think that this ancient tongue, and its rough poetry, is the last stage in his escape from everyday reality: a form of conversing in a language of his own because it is dead, forgotten, elementary.

After lunch, I took him to the National Library. We went up to his office (big, impersonal, horrible) where on a long table sat the *History of Sarmiento*, written many years ago by Leopoldo Lugones. He asked me to open it and read a page in which Lugones describes Sarmiento's house, which he had known before it was torn down. I began to read a text full of minute precisions, and almost immediately Borges took over, quoting the text from memory. He was not trying to impress me with his powers of recollection, no. After all, he knows perfectly well I have been an initiate in his growing cult for a long time. It was something else, more indirect, a way of sharing the book more actively with me, a way of participating more directly in the creation of a dream which was ours in the moment of reading but which had been Lugones' and even earlier (in mere reality) Sarmiento's own dream.

I don't want to insist too much on the allegorical content of this little episode. I just want to point out that once more, and unexpectedly, I felt myself participating in the dream of Borges' vigil: a dream created by him, with his own and others' materials, but infinitely accessible to all his readers, his collaborators, his accomplices.

Yale University

The Four Cardinal Points of Borges

By DONALD A. YATES

I.

In these brief remarks on the narrative prose of Jorge Luis Borges, I propose to attempt something at once seemingly impossible and totally obvious. Viewing the immense richness and complexity of Borges' narrative resources, one quickly perceives the apparent impossibility of describing that author's artistic orientation in a short essay. Yet like the fiction of no other contemporary writer(to judge from the growing amount of critical comment accorded to his work), Borges' prose writings invite, inspire, perhaps even demand analysis and interpretation. Thus the perfectly obvious intention of this paper.

To ascribe to Borges' artistic world four key aspects, four cardinal points, is, to be sure, arbitrary. Still, this approach need not produce necessarily invalid judgments. Schematic yes, but with any luck, in some way telling.

The narrative prose encompassed by these observations extends from "Hombres de las orillas," published in September of 1933, to "Pedro Salvadores," which appeared in the English translation of Norman Thomas di Giovanni in the *New York Review of Books* in mid-August 1969. This appearance preceded its Spanish-language publication in Jorge Luis Borges' latest collection of prose and poetry, *Elogio de la sombra*, published in Buenos Aires by Emecé on 24 August 1969—the 70th birthday of the author.

"Pedro Salvadores" is, in Borges' words, a "straightforward story" of a new type he has begun to write. The first narrative of this new style was "La intrusa," published in 1966. The general observations of this paper, I feel, apply as fully to this later narrative mood as to the above-mentioned first story by Borges (which in its subsequent appearances carries the title "Hombre de la esquina rosada"). And for those familiar with the author's more celebrated in-between stories—those of *Ficciones* and *El Aleph*—the appropriateness of these cardinal points will, I hope, be apparent.

Borges believes in the superiority of his recent narratives—"La intrusa" especially, which he now refers to as his best story, and "Pedro Salvadores," which pleases him for its simplicity. He has excused his earliest story as (again his own words) "psychologically false" and as so much "fancy work." Urged to consider that it was his first story and showed signs of having been carefully worked over and polished, he has replied, "Yes, but I think I may have overdone it."

Let us examine, then, these points of reference as they relate to Borges' fiction. They seem conveniently to characterize the stories he fashioned from his own materials—the stories of the late thirties and of the forties. But to put the theory to the test, we shall see how they apply to his latest fiction, specifically to "Pedro Salvadores," the two-page account that Borges prefers to call an anecdote, something *not* his but only recounted to him. I hope to show in some detail how, in the retelling, this episode of the Rosas terror becomes his.

II.

The cardinal points of Jorge Luis Borges are four and may be considered as corresponding to the points of the compass. Borges' south is, of course, his deeply sensed nationality as an Argentine. It is reflected not only in his literary use of Argentine settings and events, but also in the manner in which he absorbs and synthesizes borrowings from the most disparate sources. This sort of assimilation characterizes the special type of Argentine *criollismo* which must be understood in order for one to grasp the particular meaning in Argentina of the term *criollo*.

The circumstances of the author's life have combined to produce a man who, owing to chronic nearsightedness which led gradually to virtual blindness, has withdrawn from aggressive participation in the present, and has seen fit to draw drama and excitement vicariously from many sources, none perhaps more noteworthy than the participation of his ancestors in the turbulent events of his country's history. The names are woven into his pages: in the paternal line, his grandfather, Colonel Francisco Borges, whose mother, Carmen Lafinur, was sister to poet Juan Crisóstomo Lafinur whose lineage, in turn, is traced back through Gerónimo Luis de Cabrera, founder of Córdoba, to include Juan de Garay, founder of Buenos Aires after the grim failures of Juan Díaz de Solís and Pedro de Mendoza; on his mother's side, his great-grandfather, Colonel Isidro Suárez, who as an exile died during the Rosas siege of Montevideo, whose ten-year-old brother was executed by the *mazorca* at the wall of the Recoleta, and who in that young and violent land was a cousin to the despised dictator himself; a great-uncle, Francisco Narciso de Laprida, who was president of the Congress of Tucumán that initiated the movement for independence; and an uncle of Colonel Isidro Suárez, Miguel Estanislao de Soler, who was Jefe del Estado Mayor of General José de San Martín.

If Borges has any identity whatever, it is as an Argentine, and, as an American poet has expressed it, "that has made all the difference." Those who would call him "Europeanized" and criticize his indifference to Argentine reality surely understand very little about the writer and about the true meaning of the term *criollo* as applied to inhabitants of the city of his birth.

If the direction north has special significance as the principal point of orientation, then I would be inclined to say that Borges' north is most evidently language—this being extended to include its chief mode of aesthetic expression, literature, as well as the preoccupation with the techniques of that expression, literary style. Borges has stated on numerous occasions that the most significant feature of his childhood (and I have heard him extend "childhood" into "lifetime") was his father's library of English books. There is perhaps no more eloquent testimony to the truth of this statement than Borges' admission that the most vivid images that remain with him of his early years in Palermo are not of people or places or events, but of books, their feel, their smell, and the illustrations they carried. A curious statement, but one that illuminates the paths along which his life subsequently led him. His destiny, he understood at an early age, was to be a writer. And during the threescore years that have run their course since his first attempt at fashioning language—a successful translation of Oscar Wilde's story "The Happy Prince"—he has made few exceptions to a total dedication to that career.

To talk with Borges today is to relive with him and renew with him the pleasures of a life devoted to literature. Although he no longer sees and cannot read, many of those pleasures are still close to him and can be immediately recalled from the vast archive of verses—of all types and in several languages—that he has stored in his mind. At least as surprising is Borges' insistence that he has never made the slightest effort deliberately to memorize any of these lines. The beauty or felicity of the verses (or at times their exceptional badness) has sufficed to fix them in his recall. "If you have to make an effort to learn certain verses," he has said, "then they're not worth the trouble, don't you think?"

Borges' literature is made up of other literatures, and he is quick to acknowledge influences in his work. In his magical journey across a great sea of pages, he has stopped at many ports. The rich cargo he has laid aboard is a source of deep satisfaction. When his sight failed some fifteen years ago, he made a decision not to content himself with the wealth of familiarity with literature he had already acquired. He deliberately set up for himself a quest that he has pursued since 1955 and that he continues to pursue today. He took down from the upper shelves of his library a collection of books on Old English that he could no longer see, and with his students embarked on a journey back into the beginnings of that tongue which, more than any other, has enriched his life. Thus, language, in a broad, fundamental sense, continues in his later years to be a point to which he is oriented, a north by which he still guides himself.

The east of Borges' compass may be said to constitute the most distinctive feature of his writings. It could be described as a fascination with philosophical and metaphysical questions that manifests itself, in part, in the incorporation of these problems as elements of his prose fiction. His interest in these matters goes back to the philosophical works he read as a boy and discussed with his father, a teacher of psychology. In these conversations, Borges recalls, they discussed philosophical ideas on a thoroughly adult level, and his father did not treat such concepts as unusual or difficult or as requiring any more elaborate explanation than the mysteries and fantasies of the novels of Stevenson or Wells or Chesterton. In this way metaphysical problems came to form part of Borges' general reading, or literary background.

27

Following a seven-year period of education and literary apprenticeship in Switzerland and Spain, Borges returned to Buenos Aires where, waiting at the pier to welcome the family home, was his father's friend Macedonio Fernández, the man who was to influence Borges' attitude and style of thought more than any other person. With Macedonio, Borges subsequently developed an intellectual skepticism toward most commonly held beliefs of a spiritual or practical nature as well as a fondness for a personal brand of philosophic idealism that Macedonio had evolved. Together they read and discussed many books and writers in a genial tone; among them Schopenhauer, Hume, and Francis Bradley. Macedonio preferred to talk about the books he was too lazy to write. His, apparently, was an oral genius. And he had a great gift for comic invention. He was capable of saying to Borges, "Do you think we ought to commit suicide now, so as not to have to hear 'La cumparsita' played again?" Or (and this is an instance where a saying directly inspired by Macedonio was later used by and attributed to him) on describing a poorly attended lecture by an inveterate and boring speaker: "There were so few people there that if anyone else had failed to attend the lecture, he wouldn't have been able to get in."

Borges acquired many things with Macedonio Fernández, and when Borges began to write his first stories, in the late 1930s, the essentially philosophical concepts and metaphysical questions (especially those touching on time, infinity, and identity) that had been so firmly and—thanks to Macedonio—so casually assimilated as part of Borges' literary environment, were quite naturally incorporated as fictional or narrative elements of his prose. After the first two stories signed with his own name had been published—"Pierre Menard, autor del *Quijote*" and "Tlön, Uqbar, Orbis Tertius"—the narrative formula was set, and thereafter his very peculiar, very original prose style would be instantly recognizable. Borges himself, perhaps more clearly than anyone else, has described this feature of his writings, saying: "I am quite simply a man who uses perplexities for literary purposes."

The remaining point, the west of Borges' compass, is the least studied aspect of his narrative mood. James E. Irby, in a dissertation dealing with the structure of Borges' stories, touches on this feature, and other critics have talked vaguely and occasionally of the uncommon abundance of knives, swords, murders, *guapos*, *compadritos*, conspiracies, intrigues, violence, vengeance, ambushes, plots, and executions. But only recently, in Ronald Christ's *The Narrow Act*, a study of Borges' art of allusion, in the chapter entitled "The Achievement of Form," is serious attention given to what I consider the fourth and final cardinal point: the strong, ever-present narrative ingredient of drama. This element may take the form of vivid color, melodrama, mystery, or very tight clockwork plotting, but it is characteristically present in his fictions and occupies the place that, in the stories of others, would be occupied by psychological probing or exposition—features notably absent in Borges' tales.

Borges' inordinate fondness for western films, gangster movies, fantastic literature, and detective fiction (perhaps explained by the concept of psychological transference or compensation), has accounted for much of the enjoyment he has derived from everyday life. All of these interests have exerted a great influence on his writing. To begin with, he has produced in collaboration with his close friend Adolfo Bioy Casares: the don Isidro Parodi detective stories, an extravagant detective tale entitled *Un modelo para la muerte*, two Argentine gangster film scripts, two fantastic tales included in a book called *Dos fantasías memorables*, two anthologies of detective short stories, as well as a successful detective novel series (*El Séptimo Círculo*), published by Editorial Emecé. Moreover, with Bioy Casares and Silvina Ocampo he has edited a very important anthology of fantastic literature. These interests no doubt have accounted for the tone of certain of his own stories—the remarkable "La muerte y la brújula," "El jardín de senderos que se bifurcan," "Emma Zunz," "El acercamiento a Almotásim," "La espera," and others. But most significantly, his passion for fantasy and detective fiction, for gangster films, tales of *guapos, mavelos,* and *compadritos* has influenced the narrative structure of virtually all his prose fiction. Drama, usually in obvious and explicit form, is a feature of his style (we recognize him by it); moreover, it has come to represent for him a fundamental quality of the aesthetic effect he ideally hopes to achieve. It is in *Ficciones* that we find the following statement, perhaps one of the most significant formulations in all his work: "El hecho estético no puede prescindir de algún elemento de asombro."

That "asombro" is translated, in Borges' fiction, into the various forms of drama, melodrama, or sudden revelation that hold his stories firmly together. We need only recall those tales we have read to understand that the aesthetic effects Borges attains— the impression or impact they leave with the reader—are derived from the "asombro," that is, the culmination not of a single reflection or insight, but rather the discharge of narrative tension accumulated by an intricately plotted and controlled dramatic situation.

III.

Now, to test the applicability of these four features, let us turn to an example of Borges' new, "straightforward" fiction—the succinct narrative, "Pedro Salvadores," found in his latest work in Spanish, *Elogio de la sombra*. If this proposed scheme is at all valid, it should lead to a reasonably full appreciation of Borges' art as manifest in this tale. I am indebted to Norman Thomas di Giovanni for his permission to use the English translation of this story, which he has prepared in close collaboration with the author. The Spanish original has but seven paragraphs; in the English version there are eight. I shall deal exclusively with the translation.

"Pedro Salvadores" is Borges' account of a true story, a story he had heard many years before he wrote it down. In the first paragraph he states, in his own voice, two things:

> I want to leave a written record (perhaps the first to be attempted) of one of the strangest and grimmest happenings in Argentine history. To meddle as little as possible in the telling, to abstain from picturesque details or personal conjectures is, it seems to me, the only way to do this.

Here we have two quite different aspects. There is starkness and honesty in the author's intention to leave "a written record" of this incident (such, of course, is the function of prose), and the professed determination to accomplish this without descending to "fancy writing" is both disarming and subtly deceptive. But we are drawn closer by a promise of drama—the relating of "one of the strangest and grimmest happenings in Argentine history." In one paragraph, two sentences, three of the four aspects discussed above are evoked. The fourth, the author's concern with philosophical ideas, quickly comes into play in the next expository paragraph. Here we are given once more a forthright look into the narrator's art; like the magician before his trick, Borges shows us his hand, seeming to fulfill the promise he has just made: "A man, a woman, and the overpowering shadow of a dictator are the three characters. The man's name was Pedro Salvadores; my grandfather Acevedo saw him days or weeks after the dictator's downfall in the battle of Caseros." In these lines Borges proceeds directly to the telling of the story he has announced; and a key element in the structure of the inner narrative has been inserted (as we shall see) in the reference to the meeting between Borges' grandfather and Pedro Salvadores.

Next appears the first feature of a philosophical nature—a brief allusion to the concept of destiny, and the casual evocation of the question of identity, which the author will develop more fully near the story's end: "Pedro Salvadores may have been no different from anyone else, but the years and his fate set him apart." The paragraph continues, providing, in terms as succinct as those in which the cast of characters was presented, the setting of the story. The scene of the events is suggested as being as typically anonymous as Salvadores is himself:

> He was a gentleman like many gentlemen of his day. He owned (let us suppose) a ranch in the country and, opposed to the tyranny, was on the Unitarian side. His wife's family name was Planes; they lived together on Suipacha Street near the corner of Temple in what is now the heart of Buenos Aires. The house in which the event took place was much like any other, with its street door, long arched entrance-way, inner grillwork gate, its rooms, its row of two or three patios. The dictator, of course, was Rosas.

Now the stage is set and the announced drama begins. In the next paragraph the only violent incidents of the story occur. The sparse and unembellished account of the rapid series of happenings both fulfills the author's promise "to abstain from picturesque details" and reflects a cinematographic narrative technique that Borges has used success-fully before (e.g., in "Hombre de la esquina rosada").

> One night, around 1842, Salvadores and his wife heard the growing, muffled sound of horses' hooves out on the unpaved street and the riders shouting their drunken *vivas* and their threats. This time Rosas' henchmen did not ride on. After the shouts came repeated knocks at the door; while the men began forcing it, Salvadores was able to pull the dining-room table aside, lift the rug, and hide himself down in the cellar. His wife dragged the table back in place. The *mazorca* broke into the house; they had come to take Salvadores. The woman said her husband had run away to Montevideo. The men did not believe her; they flogged her,

they smashed all the blue chinaware (blue was the Unitarian color), they searched the whole house, but they never thought of lifting the rug. At midnight they rode away, swearing that they would soon be back.

There now occurs a curious paragraph. While it contains necessary information, it is the least effective of the entire story. For this, I think, there is a reason. Something must be said about Salvadores here (the next paragraph will deal with his wife). Yet after the period of his confinement is specified there is little Borges tells about Salvadores' underground existence—that is, until he is ready to consider, from a philosophical viewpoint, what the meaning of Salvadores' adventure might be. And this will not occur until two paragraphs later. The conclusion we may draw from this is that the details of Salvadores' confinement interest Borges much less than the conjectures he might draw from it or the interpretation he might suggest for it. This, of course, coincides with the scheme of narrative values we have discussed. The paragraph is as follows:

> Here is the true beginning of Pedro Salvadores' story. He lived nine years in the cellar. For all we may tell ourselves that years are made of days and days of hours and that nine years is an abstract term and an impossible sum, the story is nonetheless gruesome. I suppose that in the darkness, which his eyes somehow learned to decipher, he had no particular thoughts, not even of his hatred or his danger. He was simply there—in the cellar—with echoes of the world he was cut off from sometimes reaching him from overhead: his wife's footsteps, the bucket clanging against the lip of the well, a heavy rainfall in the patio. Every day of his imprisonment, for all he knew, could have been the last.

But now comes a masterful paragraph. In half a dozen lines Borges relates the nine-year tribulation of Salvadores' wife. He has compressed into these few lines, still abstaining from "picturesque details or personal conjecture," the image of an extraordinary woman, all the facts we need to know about her life during the nine years, and an arresting and almost gratuitous dramatic surprise:

> His wife let go all the servants, who could possibly have informed against them, and told her family that Salvadores was in Uruguay. Meanwhile, she earned a living for them both sewing uniforms for the army. In the course of time, she gave birth to two children; her family turned from her, thinking she had a lover. After the tyrant's fall, they got down on their knees and begged to be forgiven.

The last sentence breaks the time sequence because the balance of the story is about Salvadores, and his wife's situation needs to be resolved here before we return to his experience.

The next paragraph is the justification, in Borges' eyes, for the narrative. In it he searches, characteristically, for the possible significance behind the facts. The questions that begin the paragraph, even after Borges gives them extended consideration, remain unanswered at the end. And it is out of this final perplexity that Borges, a few lines later, draws the story's concluding reflection. In this "justifying" paragraph we observe the limpid, precise language and the poised, perceptive, but fundamentally interrogative attitude that, in turn, justify Borges to his reader:

What was Pedro Salvadores? Who was he? Was it his fear, his love, the unseen presence of Buenos Aires, or—in the long run—habit that held him prisoner? In order to keep him with her, his wife would make up news to tell him about whispered plots and rumored victories. Maybe he was a coward and she loyally hid it from him that she knew. I picture him in his cellar perhaps without a candle, without a book. Darkness probably sank him into sleep. His dreams, at the outset, were probably of that sudden night when the blade sought his throat, of the streets he knew so well, of the open plains. As the years went on, he would have been unable to escape even in his sleep; whatever he dreamed would have taken place in the cellar. At first, he may have been a man hunted down, a man in danger of his life; later (we will never know for certain), an animal at peace in its burrow or a sort of dim god.

The final sentence of the story is properly a part of the paragraph just cited. But Borges withholds it, with considerable effect, while he occupies himself with resolving the external structure of the narrative. Now we have a reference to the encounter between Borges' grandfather and Salvadores that was prefigured at the story's beginning. The balance of the brief paragraph generates a calculated falling, anticlimactic tone, which provides the necessary contrast with the story's last sentence:

All this went on until that summer day of 1852 when Rosas fled the country. It was only then that the secret man came out into the light of day; my grandfather spoke with him. Flabby, overweight, Salvadores was the color of wax and could not speak above a low voice. He never got back his confiscated lands; I think he died in poverty.

Now the final element of the tale: "As with so many things, the fate of Pedro Salvadores strikes us as a symbol of something we are about to understand, but never quite do." Close readers of Borges will perceive a familiar ring in this final line. It is a lucidly expressed insight and, of course, echoes the closing lines of Borges' essay (included in *Otras inquisiciones*), "The Wall and the Books," which reads as follows:

Music, states of happiness, mythology, faces belabored by time, certain twilights and certain places try to tell us something, or have said something we should not have missed, or are about to say something; this imminence of revelation which does not occur is, perhaps the aesthetic phenomenon.

IV.

I hope it is clear that in "Pedro Salvadores" Borges blends the four aspects we have discussed into a prose narrative in which we cannot fail to sense the presence of his hand. The consciousness of his Argentine nationality, his acute awareness of language and the theory and practice of literary art, his persistent artistic concern with the perplexities of philosophical and metaphysical speculation, and his highly developed appreciation of the essence of drama are surely all present and apparent in this story. It may even be said that they constitute the principal ingredients of the prose style of Jorge Luis Borges.

I wish now to express my profound admiration for the man, seated here with us, who, because of his special gifts and because he frequented for so many years the great and memorable books and writers of all time, has, I think, somehow become contaminated by immortality.

Michigan State University

Borges and the Idea of Utopia

By JAMES E. IRBY

> *Il n'y a pas de hors-texte.*
> Jacques Derrida, *De la grammatologie*
> . . . *ce lieu obscur qui ne songe interminablement qu'à se déchiffrer.*
> Jean Ricardou, *Problèmes du nouveau roman*

Toward the end of 1938, under circumstances he has told in interviews and fictionalized in his story "El Sur," Borges nearly died of septicemia. This delirious ordeal, which also caused him to fear for his sanity, soon was revealed, however, as an incredible stroke of good fortune. Prompted by a desperate resolve to test his mental capacity, the convalescent Borges undertook to write something in a new genre, to write—as he said later—"something new and different for me, so that I could blame the novelty of the effort if I failed."[1] This new work was the story "Pierre Menard, autor del Quijote," the first of a rich and dazzling series of metaphysical tales with which, after some years of relatively scant and tentative writings, Borges did considerably more than just reaffirm his creative powers. In May 1939, "Pierre Menard, autor del Quijote" was published in Victoria Ocampo's review *Sur*. Exactly one year later, in the same journal, appeared the next such tale, "Tlön, Uqbar, Orbis Tertius," which subsequently opened the volumes *El jardín de senderos que se bifurcan* (1941) and *Ficciones* (1944). This leading position was not, therefore, a matter of chronological but rather of theoretical priority, for perhaps more fully than any other of his fictions, it declares their basic principles, characteristically making of that declaration a fictionalized essay, a creation which studies itself. The subject, fittingly enough, is the enigmatic emergence of a new man-made universe, systematically designed and inserted into reality. For this reason, and for other reasons I will mention shortly, I would like to discuss this work in relation to the idea of utopia. My discussion will be divided into three parts: (1) some of the senses in which the world of Tlön is a utopia, (2) some anticipations of this idea in Borges' earlier writings, and (3) some of the ways in which the presentation of Tlön is dramatized. But first, a reminder of the tale's plot.

I.

In a kind of memoir mingling essayistic discourse with anecdote, real names with inventions, Borges tells how his friend Bioy Casares discovers in an anomalous copy of a pirated edition of the *Encyclopaedia Britannica* an interpolated entry on a supposed country in Asia Minor called Uqbar, which diligent consultations elsewhere fail to verify. The entry mentions that the epics and legends of Uqbar never refer to reality but to the imaginary regions of Mlejnas and Tlön. Later Borges himself comes upon the eleventh volume of a so-called *First Encyclopaedia of Tlön*, which bears the unexplained inscription "Orbis Tertius" and contains fragmentary though methodical information on what is now said to be an entire planet. Astonished and delighted like a true bibliophile, after referring to various friends' polemics over the dubious existence of the other volumes and to vulgar distortions by the popular press, all of which the reader is presumed to recall, Borges proceeds to outline the *Weltanschauung* of this "brave new world."

Whereas our common concept of reality is materialistic, i.e. presupposes the independent existence of material objects and beings that the mind registers like a camera, Tlön's universal philosophy is a kind of ultra-Berkeleyan idealism according to which the only realities are mental perceptions. Not even space exists, only a dimensionless continuum of thought. This is first exemplified in an account of the planet's languages, which determine the nature of all its disciplines. In Tlön there are no nouns, only adjectives (qualities) or verbs (acts or processes), variable aggregates of which may comprise the entities designated by our nouns, and countless other entities as well. Both these and other constructs ranging all the way from causal links to scientific or theological systems are completely metaphorical, are "poetic objects," since only instantaneous perceptions are real, not their subsequent connections in memory. Hence in Tlön philosophies proliferate and compete wildly like avant-garde poetic styles, although the hypothesis that the universe is one supreme mind, that all phenomena are the somehow-associated thoughts of that mind, seems to prevail. The most scandalous heresy in Tlön is, of course, materialism, which the languages of Tlön can scarcely even formulate as an *aporia*. Borges' summary of this world concludes with a dizzying account of how its "things" multiply by thought and, conversely, vanish when they are forgotten.

To the sections on Uqbar and Tlön, Borges adds a concluding postscript already dated "1947" in the original 1940.[2] Here curious discovery and eager discussion give way to a somewhat troubled report that Tlön has begun to intrude into our own everyday world. A letter discovered by chance reveals the history of its laborious creation over a period of centuries by anonymous groups of scholars, first in Europe, later in the New World. Strange objects from Tlön are found, the entire *First Encyclopaedia* is unearthed and widely excerpted, and everywhere people yield to the enchantment of an orderly, man-made universe of the mind come to supplant the divinely incomprehensible reality we know. One by one our sciences are reformed, our very memories replaced by others. In a hundred years, a projected *Second Encyclopaedia* will appear, announcing the even more ample but as yet undefined realm of Orbis Tertius, by which time our world will already be Tlön. As these events unfold, Borges finally assumes a resigned indifference, idly correcting his never to be published translation of Sir Thomas Browne's *Urn Burial*, which the advent of Tlön and its marvellous tongues will surely obliterate.

All this, rich with enticing allusion and ellipsis, is compressed into some twenty-odd pages. Even in rapid synopsis one can see that "Tlön, Uqbar, Orbis Tertius" comprises many interwoven levels of meaning whose relationships alone are exceedingly complex, not to speak of the levels themselves. Already a kind of palimpsest, a many-layered paraphrase of other paraphrases, the tale tends to make any critical résumé and commentary both desperately tautological and inaccurate, for at every turn one is also faced with sly reversals and subversions of the very schemes the work sets forth. For the moment, however, let us assume that, at least insofar as exposition is concerned, there are two main levels, one being that of the narrator's own progressive involvement with the events he relates, and the other (contained within the first) being that of the description and chronicle of Tlön itself.

The theoretical section of this second level (the summary of the Eleventh Volume) offers the outlines of a special kind of utopia, a most pure and extreme utopia, so to speak. Here is no new social order, but rather a new natural order, a whole new epistemology, a new relationship between mind and phenomena, worked out in myriad consequences of detail. Furthermore, this is done not in some single futuristic *roman de moeurs*, but in a vast, many-volumed compendium which registers not only the science and mathematics, the languages and literary theory, of an idealist cosmos, but also (according to certain oblique references by the narrator) its no doubt singular flora and fauna, topography and architecture. Literally, Tlön is an *ideal* world (a world of ideas) and a *utopia* (a no place, a world outside spatial coordinates). In its denial of matter, it constitutes a drastic case of what all utopias imply: the world upside down, a mirror image of habitual reality. (Remember the tale's first sentence: "I owe the discovery of Uqbar to the conjunction of a mirror and an encyclopedia."[3]) This paradox (etymologically the word "paradox" means "contrary to opinion," that is, to ordinary opinion) is paralleled by another which also relates to an essential aspect of utopia. Utopias represent a convergence of reason and reality and are presumably objects of desire. In Tlön thought and reality are *one*, but desire or hope or even distraction may engender more or less faithful *duplicates* of anything (or duplicates of duplicates, and so on). These are known as *hrönir*, which, among other properties, have a profound temporal effect. In the narrator's incomparable words:

> The methodical fabrication of *hrönir* . . . has performed prodigious services for archaeologists. It has made possible the interrogation and even the modification of the past, which is now no less plastic and docile than the future.[4]

He then points out the delicate differences between *hrönir* of various degrees: "those of fifth degree are almost uniform; those of ninth degree become confused with those of the second; in those of the eleventh there is a purity of line not found in the original."[5]

At this point, as it draws to a close, the whole scholarly review of the Eleventh Volume works up to a wild crisis beneath its calm, detached language. The idea of proliferation, of the endless rivalry and replacement of unverifiable mental constructs, was earlier introduced by referring to theories; now it operates with pencils, rusty wheels, gold masks, buildings. The gradual shift in vocabulary to familiar terms we construe as "concrete" forces us with growing perplexity to realize what is happening, to read these passages over and over, i.e. to produce our own succession of textual *hrönir*. Furthermore, it would seem that in a world where supposedly "a later state of the subject . . . cannot affect or illuminate the previous state,"[6] forms and moments nevertheless minutely substitute for one another in a headlong rush toward indistinguishability, toward chaos. And yet, we are told, this world has been codified in an encyclopedia, this spaceless world divided into northern and southern hemispheres.

The narrator caps his summary of the Eleventh Volume with a very brief description of how objects fade and disappear *from view* when forgotten. The idea of proliferation is thus abruptly juxtaposed with that of loss, and, retroactively, the idea of forgetting suggests that the preceding discussion of *hrönir* was, at least in part, an extended metaphor of the processes of memory, as well as of historiography. In his recent conversations with Richard Burgin, Borges recalls how, when a child, he heard his father speak of his own childhood memories as only memories of other memories, like a pile of coins each of whose effigies imperceptibly distorts the one before, moving further and further away from the now-unknown original.[7] This "saddening thought," already a contradictory union of proliferation and loss like the idea of the *hrönir*, is also found on a magnified scale at the end of "Tlön, Uqbar, Orbis Tertius."

Borges' utopia is an idealistic one because that philosophy represents, for him, a victory of mind over matter, over the "hard and fast," over all inert resistance and unreason. But his uncanny pursuit of its ultimate consequences, logically discarding Berkeley's coherence-lending God, swirls toward a total atomization where reason finds no foothold.[8] Already in its discursive middle section we begin to experience the story's essential drama and can glimpse at least three implications: (1) intensifying the paradox of Tlön enlarges its scope to parallel or include our perception of the story itself, (2) Tlön is also a nightmare, an "anti-utopia," and (3) its states are not so fantastic or otherworldly after all. Perhaps I can make this more clear by showing how the main levels of the story interact, particularly in the very moving (and ambiguous) final pages. But first, I would like to trace some of the intimations of utopia in previous works by Borges.

II.

Borges began his literary career around 1920 as an affiliate, first in Spain, later in Buenos Aires, of the so-called *ultraísta* movement, an enthusiastic but rather incoherent version of futurism which exalted the juxtaposition of violent metaphors as the sole poetic device. Borges, however, far from incoherent, tried to establish in his own manifestos and essays of the period a theory of metaphor based on clear philosophical principles. These writings repeatedly display three themes: (1) the use of Berkeleyan idealism to break down substantive reality—and even the continuities of space and personal identity—into a flux of immediate perceptions, (2) the combinational rearrangement of these perceptions by means of metaphor to form new poetic realities, and (3) the fervent hope that the future would bring a collective realization of his theories.

Argentine *ultraísmo* quickly evolved into another more nationalistically inspired movement now usually termed *martinfierrismo* (after its principal review, *Martín Fierro*), in which Borges also figured prominently. Now his futuristic vision ("futuristic" in the literal sense) also embraced a desire for a more lucid and authentic national literature, centered (for him) on images of the old quarters of his beloved Buenos Aires. The title essay of his book *El tamaño de mi esperanza* (1926) exhorts his companions to join him in that task:

> Now Buenos Aires, more than a city, is a country, and we must find the poetry and the music and the painting and the religion and the metaphysics that correspond to its greatness. That is the magnitude of my hope, which invites us all to be gods and work toward its incarnation.[9]

Here we can already glimpse something of the demiurgical, collective, and encyclopedic enterprise that engenders Tlön.

Another essay in the same volume, "Palabrería para versos," outlines his concurrent and admittedly utopian aspiration toward a language of new and more comprehensive signs:

> The world of appearances is a rush of jumbled perceptions. . . . Language is an effective arrangement of the world's enigmatic abundance. In other words, with our nouns we invent realities. We touch a round form, we see a glob of dawn-colored light, a tickle delights our mouth, and we falsely say these three heterogeneous things are one, known as an orange. The moon itself is a fiction. . . . All nouns are abbreviations. . . . The world of appearances is most complex and our language has realized only a very small number of the combinations which it allows. Why not create a word, one single word, for our simultaneous perception of cattle bells ringing in the afternoon and the sunset in the distance? . . . I know how utopian my ideas are and how far it is from an intellectual possibility to a real one, but I trust in the magnitude of the future and that it will be no less ample than my hope.[10]

This, of course, reads like a preliminary draft for the section on language and "poetic objects" in "Tlön, Uqbar, Orbis Tertius," and is, in turn, a revision of passages from earlier *ultraísta* writings. All of these texts, placed side by side, suggest an essential oneness, a Janus-faced sense of time which in fact Borges often invoked in the 1920s by defining hope as "memory of the future"[11] or "recollection coming to us from the future."[12]

By 1930 the boom period of avant-garde solidarity and national optimism was over. The tone and concerns of Borges' work shifted, though not its underlying premises and implications. In a little-known address given in 1936 on the occasion of the four hundredth anniversary of Buenos Aires, he now spoke with uncertain pathos of his native city's mushrooming growth as a sacrifice of past and present in the name of an unknown future which hope must nevertheless somehow welcome:

> No one feels time and the past like a native of Buenos Aires. . . . He knows he lives in a city which grows like a tree, like a familiar face in a nightmare. . . . In this corner of America . . . men from all nations have made a pact to disappear

for the sake of a new man which is none of us yet . . . . A most singular pact, an extravagant adventure of races, not to survive but to be in the end forgotten: lineages seeking darkness. [. . .] Buenos Aires imposes upon us the terrible obligation of hope. Upon all of us it imposes a strange love—a love of the secret future and its unknown face.[13]

In those years Borges had abandoned poetry and ceased to theorize about metaphor, turning instead to the problem of fiction, whose aims and devices he first examined in the volume of essays called *Discusión* (1932), one of his most fascinating and unjustly neglected works. His earlier essays had brightly proposed a salutary reduction of common realities to an immediate swarm of perceptions. In *Discusión*, however, such a state lurks as a perplexing disorder to be resolved not by metaphors or a new poetic vocabulary but by a linear discourse of oblique allusions and internal correspondences which "postulate" a coherent reality existing only by virtue of the text itself. In a key essay entitled precisely "La postulación de la realidad," Borges argues this in a most devious fashion, mingling as specimens both historical and literary texts, leaving his reader to deduce for himself that *all* discourse is "fictional." Another key essay, "El arte narrativo y la magia," concludes that imaginative or fantastic fiction is superior to other kinds because of its broader, "magical" notion of causality, linking elements by similarity and contiguity as well as by logical cause and effect.

Discusión is also the first of Borges' works to include essays of a type quite frequent in his later writings: examinations of fantastic cosmologies—the cabbala, gnosticism and (ironically, critically juxtaposed with these) the Christian conception of Hell—which, of course, are also "fictions." His interest in such theories suggests one of the reasons why Borges turned from poetry to narrative in those years: a need to treat in more dramatic form questions of human destiny, of time, illusion, and finality, and to do so within some closely reasoned world picture radically opposed to unthinking mental habit.

Another model or symbol of this enterprise was the concept of utopia, scarcely mentioned in *Discusión*,[14] but emphatically used a few years later to invoke an ideal of pure, thorough inventiveness which most fantastic literature neglected. In March 1936 he opened his review of an early volume of stories by Bioy Casares with words which anticipate the subject of "Tlön, Uqbar, Orbis Tertius" and one of the story's passages:

> I suspect that a general scrutiny of fantastic literature would reveal that it is not very fantastic. I have visited many Utopias—from the eponymous one of More to *Brave New World*—and I have not yet found a single one that exceeds the cozy limits of satire or sermon and describes in detail an imaginary country, with its geography, its history, its religion, its language, its literature, its music, its government, its metaphysical and theological controversy . . . its encyclopedia, in short; all of it organically coherent, of course, and (I know I'm very demanding) with no reference whatsoever to the horrible injustices suffered by captain Alfred Dreyfus.[15]

There is one more direct anticipation of "Tlön, Uqbar, Orbis Tertius" worthy of note, this time in the nature of a formal prototype which not only parodied both Borges' avant-garde theories and (before the fact) his ideas on fiction, but also showed how intimately a mad drive toward total disruption could coexist with his dreams of order. This prototype was revealed a few years ago in his remarkable preface to an anthology of writings by his late friend and mentor Macedonio Fernández (1874–1952). Onetime anarchist, genial eccentric, a kind of Charles Ives of Argentine metaphysics who improvised vast idealist negations of time and self, Macedonio became for the young *martinfierristas* a guiding spirit in disinterested speculation and absurd humor and was, in Borges' words, "the most extraordinary man I've ever known."[16]

One of Macedonio's most curious fantasies was that of becoming president of Argentina, a goal toward which he felt he should first move by very subtly insinuating his name to the populace. Presumably sometime in the 1920s, Borges and a number of friends undertook collectively to write and place themselves as characters in a novel enlarging upon these imaginary machinations, a work to be entitled "El hombre que será presidente," of which only the two opening chapters were composed. The obvious plot, relating Macedonio's efforts, all but concealed another, concerning the conspiracy of a group of "neurotic and perhaps insane millionaires"[17] to further the same campaign by undermining people's resistance through the gradual dissemination of "disturbing inventions."[18] These were usually contradictory artefacts whose effect ran counter to their apparent form or function, including certain very small and disconcertingly heavy objects (like the cone found by Borges and Amorim toward the end of "Tlön, Uqbar, Orbis Tertius"), scrambled passages in detective novels (somewhat like the interpolated entry on Uqbar), and dadaist creations (perhaps like the "transparent tigers" and "towers of blood" in Tlön). The novel's technique and language were meant to enact as well as relate this whole process by introducing more and more such objects in a less and less casual way and by slowly gravitating toward a baroque style of utter delirium. In the end, Macedonio was in fact to reach the Casa Rosada, but, as Borges adds, "by then nothing means anything in that anarchical world."[19] From this project for an idealist's devastating rise to power, let us return to the story of Tlön.

III.

Borges' outline of "El hombre que será presidente" points up what is also one of the most striking formal aspects of "Tlön, Uqbar, Orbis Tertius": the mirroring of plot elements in the verbal texture of the tale. Consider, for example, Tlön's emergence. Within the story this comes about through a growing series of textual substitutions, ambiguities, revisions, and cross references which engender a whole new state of affairs and even seem to elicit rather palpable objects (more about these later). Borges' own text comprises an intricate network of word choices and juxtapositions that almost imperceptibly operate in a similar fashion. There is, of course, the mingling of real and invented names, and the narrator's self-revision in the postscript even as the *First Encyclopaedia* is revised in its second appearance. There are the word shifts I mentioned earlier, and others as well: at times a few adjectives seem to generate new degrees of "reality," one at the expense of the other. When Borges discovers the Eleventh Volume,

41

the hitherto merely dubious Uqbar becomes "a nonexistent country" alongside the designation of Tlön as "an unknown planet"; [20] later, however, Tlön is called "an illusory world"[21] to make way for the "still nebulous Orbis Tertius."[22] Very tenuous or even omitted indications can be curiously evocative. The name "Orbis Tertius" first appears in the Eleventh Volume stamped on "a leaf of silk paper that covered one of the color plates"; [23] this subordinate allusion to a veiled image makes the volume and the name more vivid; later one may well wonder what manner of "thing" could be pictured there. In the postscript, we learn of the slave-owning, freethinking American millionaire Ezra Buckley and his role in enlarging the secret society's project to the creation of an entire planet, for all must be on a grand scale in America.[24] This episode culminates with an abrupt syntactical leap: "Buckley was poisoned in Baton Rouge in 1828; in 1914 the society delivered to its collaborators, some three hundred in number, the last volume of the First Encyclopedia of Tlön."[25] Filling in the dark gap between these two statements, following up other hints, parallels Alfonso Reyes' alleged proposal that Borges and his friends reconstruct the Eleventh Volume's missing companions *ex ungue leonem*, a proposal which, in turn, adumbrates a basic principle of Tlön: mental projection. The very first elements in the story—the mirror, the duplicated yet "false" encyclopedia, the debated narrative whose omissions or inconsistencies (not its direct statements) allow one to *guess* its "atrocious or banal" subject—set this process in motion by reflecting one another in widening patterns of self-reference. Indeed they signal that this is a text about its own principles, about the principles of all texts. Tlön is also the world of writing, of *escritura*, which consists in the meaningful permutation and alignment of signs according to inherent laws and not in the mere transcription of some prior, nonverbal reality.[26]

The chronicle of Tlön can also be seen as a partial allegory of the emergence of Borges' own fiction over the years. The narrator's involvement with the events indicates, first of all, that Borges views his work as something revealed to him, as the heritage of many other writings over the centuries, the interplay of many more or less related texts animated by a suprapersonal spirit, with himself, Borges, serving only as their momentary reader. This conception that the literary work is really generated by the interaction of other works "dans l'espace sans frontières de la lecture"—a conception reflected in the critical theories of Tlön, in the creative method of Pierre Menard, in the essays of *Otras inquisiciones*—constitutes what Gérard Genette has called Borges' "literary utopia."[27] But why do the last two pages of the tale so strangely combine notes of triumph and doubt, why does the narrator turn away at the end?

In his radio interviews with Georges Charbonnier in 1965, Borges said that all his stories are in the manner of games with two aspects, two sides of the same coin, one comprising the intellectual possibilities of a cosmic idea, the other the emotions of anguish and perplexity in the face of the endless universe. He added that any work, in order to last, must allow variable readings.[28] In a conversation with me two years later, referring specifically to "Tlön, Uqbar, Orbis Tertius," Borges stressed this story's emotional side, which he defined as "the dismay of the teller, who feels that his everyday world . . . , his past . . . [and] the past of his forefathers . . . [are] slipping away from him." Hence, he claimed, "the subject is not Uqbar or Orbis Tertius but rather a man who is being drowned in a new and overwhelming world that he can hardly make out."[29]

As the story concludes, Tlön does far more than win great droves of converts: it assumes all the obliterating scope and impetus of historical change itself, virtually annihilating the narrator, who in a hundred years, when the full transformation of our world occurs, will long be dead. Here again is the effect of simultaneous proliferation and loss. Hence the pathos of "I pay no attention to all this," the irony of translating *Urn Burial*, that magnificent set of baroque paradoxes on immortality. "Tlön, Uqbar, Orbis Tertius" is the first of a number of Borges' fictions which place an image of himself (to use Kierkegaard's phrase) "as a vanishing peculiarity in connection with the absolute requirement"[30]: Borges and the Aleph, Borges and the Zahir, Borges and the fate of Pedro Damián. This "sacrifice" lends poignant urgency to the new order enveloping him, or rather it visibly culminates an insinuation that has grown throughout the work: the mental powers, vicissitudes and vertigos of Tlön are *our own world*, our world of reality as shifting symbol, of relentless time and unknown ultimate pattern, here paradoxically turned about and fabled to help us perceive it more acutely as such. (This, by the way, would explain the words "atrocious or banal" at the beginning.) Northrop Frye has observed that all utopias present "unconscious mental habits transposed into their conscious equivalents."[31] Borges concludes one list of Tlön's inroads with the words "already a fictitious past occupies in our memories the place of another, a past of which we know nothing with certainty—not even that it is false,"[32] a peril of all recollection, as the *hrönir* implied, as well as an ironic reference to the feigned memoir we are being offered.

Tlön grows by revisions toward a "third orb" (which in turn implies a fourth and a fifth and so on), sprawling like some horrible map aspiring to coincide totally with the incalculable terrain it set out to represent within manageable coordinates on another plane. But this same self-revision can also be seen as the difficult virtue of a world of lucid thought, of multiple views. Gérard Genot, in his little book on Borges, believes that the narrator's lack of attention at the end signifies a loss of interest, because Tlön, now "real," has fallen from its former wealth of fictive potentialities. To this I would reply that the narrator may be rejecting what he has repeatedly noted to be a vulgarization of Tlön by the general public, who confuse its games with some kind of sacred order (a clear warning to readers and critics), and that Tlön clearly continues to evolve (in our minds). Genot goes on to observe, however, that the narrator's refuge in translation only confirms the extent of Tlön's influence, for the union of such disparate figures as Quevedo and Sir Thomas Browne into one text is but another version of its critical practices.[33] Frances Weber, in her article on fiction and philosophy in Borges, claims that Tlön negates itself by replacing its variable theories and countertheories with an inflexible totalitarian order to enter our world. Again I would point to the popular misconceptions and continuing change, but I fully agree with the conclusions she draws from

43

this and other stories: they are all "self-reversing tales" in which initially opposing factors coalesce and dissolve by a process of "negative thinking" that keeps us "aware of the conjectural character of all knowledge and all representation."[34] The central focus we sense but cannot grasp in the midst of all these painful and playful contrapositions might be the true utopia, the true "no place," the supreme fiction.

Princeton University

[1] James E. Irby, "Encuentro con Borges," *Revista de la Universidad de México*, XVI, no. 10, June 1962, p. 8.

[2] Then the opening words of the postscript were "I reproduce the preceding article just as it appeared in number 68 of *Sur*—jade green covers, May 1940," i.e. the very issue the reader held in his hands: an interesting *mise en abime* Borges had to renounce when the tale was reprinted in book form.

[3] *Labyrinths*, Norfolk, 1962, p. 3.

[4] *Ibid.*, p. 14.

[5] *Ibid.*

[6] *Ibid.*, pp. 9–10.

[7] Richard Burgin, *Conversations with Jorge Luis Borges*, New York, 1969, pp. 10–11. Perhaps this intricately genetic memory is not unrelated to the statement which at the beginning of the tale Bioy remembers (and modifies) from the spurious encyclopedia: "Mirrors and fatherhood are abominable because they multiply and disseminate . . . [the] universe" (*Labyrinths*, p. 4).

[8] See in Burgin, pp. 142–43, Borges' preference for the "haziness" of philosophy over "hard and fast things." See also, in *Labyrinths*, both his espousal of idealism's unreality (pp. 207–208) and his recognition of its chaos (p. 221).

[9] *El tamaño de mi esperanza*, Buenos Aires, 1926, p. 9.

[10] *Ibid.*, pp. 45–46, 48–49.

[11] *Ibid.*, p. 5.

[12] *El idioma de los argentinos*, Buenos Aires, 1928, p. 183.

[13] "Tareas y destino de Buenos Aires," *Homenaje a Buenos Aires en el cuarto centenario de su fundación*, Buenos Aires, 1936, pp. 530–31.

[14] On the constructive effect of nonspecification, he writes: "how admirable that Thomas More's first remark about Utopia should be his perplexed ignorance of how long one of its bridges 'really' is" (*Discusión*, 2nd ed., Buenos Aires, 1957, p. 70).

[15] "Adolfo Bioy Casares: La estatua casera," *Sur*, no. 18, March 1936, p. 85.

[16] *Macedonio Fernández*, Buenos Aires, 1961, p. 15.

[17] *Ibid.*, p. 18.

[18] *Ibid.*, p. 19.

[19] *Ibid.*

[20] *Labyrinths*, p. 7.

[21] *Ibid.*, p. 15.

[22] *Ibid.*, p. 17.

[23] *Ibid.*, p. 7.

[24] It is interesting to recall that Bishop Berkeley harbored the utopian dream of founding a university in the New World to propagate his philosophy unfettered by European prejudice, a plan unrealized for lack of funds. Note also the slightly distorted reflection of the name "Berkeley" in "Buckley," the sordid millions behind the ideal cause, the atheist's desire to offer God a rival creation, the faint echoes of Lazarus Morell's sinister schemes in *Historia universal de la infamia*.

[25] *Labyrinths*, p. 15.

[26] When at last Tlön appears by way of "things" rather than texts—the compass and the cone—these turn out to be signs so elaborately involved in a system of *simpatías y diferencias* that their ultimate referent seems to be that system itself. Both indicate unseen forces, the compass pointing to our magnetic north, the cone standing for the divinity in certain religions of Tlön. Both are circular metallic artefacts, one light and vibrant, the other exceedingly dense and inert. Both are paradoxically composite, the compass designating our directions with letters from Tlön, the cone not only combining very small size with enormous weight but also posing the even greater paradox of such ponderous matter emanating from an immaterial world. (This ironic inversion of our long standing verbal habit of conceiving the divine as purely spiritual recalls Olaf Stapledon's science fiction novel, *Last and First Men*, where cloudlike Martians venerate diamonds. See Borges' note on this work in *El Hogar*, 23 July 1937, p. 30.) Such a composite nature stresses the fact that all objects, all nouns, are precarious bundles of qualities which both attract and repel one another. Just as an apocryphal text is found interpolated into a known encyclopedia at the beginning of the tale, the compass and the cone are found amid various familiar objects which lend them a certain plausibility. Moreover, the network of their attributes is woven into the classic Argentine polarity between Buenos Aires and the hinterland, which in turn suggests civilization and barbarity, Europe and the New World, past and future, et cetera. Readers sometimes assume that the compass and the cone (especially the latter) are *hrönir*, an assumption nowhere substantiated in the tale but which reflects these two objects' seeming

emergence from the preceding discussion of mental duplication and from the series of more and more "concrete" references. It should also be noted, however, that the compass and the cone, coming between Erfjord's letter and the complete First Encyclopedia, are subordinated to a larger, continuing series of varying texts (including and growing out of Borges' own, of course), and that it is these which finally impress the public and transform the world.

27 Gérard Genette, "L'utopie littéraire," in his *Figures*, Paris, 1966, pp. 123–32.

28 Georges Charbonnier, *Entretiens avec Jorge Luis Borges*, Paris, 1967, pp. 20–21, 132–33.

29 Conversation recorded in Cambridge, Massachusetts, 17 November 1967. Upon discovering the Eleventh Volume, the narrator says he will not describe his feelings, "for this is not the story of my emotions but of Uqbar and Tlön and Orbis Tertius," but he then proceeds to suggest their nature by means of a mystical metaphor (*Labyrinths*, pp. 6–7).

30 Søren Kierkegaard, *Concluding Unscientific Postscript*, Princeton, 1944, p. 449.

31 Northrop Frye, "Varieties of Literary Utopias," *Daedalus*, Spring 1965, p. 325.

32 *Labyrinths*, p. 18.

33 Gérard Genot, *Borges*, Florence, 1969, pp. 33–34.

34 Frances Wyers Weber, "Borges' Stories: Fiction and Philosophy," *Hispanic Review*, vol. XXXVI, no. 2, April 1968, pp. 126, 139, 140–41.

Oxymoronic Structure
In Borges' Essays

By JAIME ALAZRAKI

Borges the fiction writer and poet has been a subject of greater appeal and interest for critics than Borges the essayist. Among the twenty-odd books dealing with his work, and throughout extensive periodical criticism, his essays are presented and discussed not as a separate genre but rather as "a necessary complement to the stories of *Ficciones* and *El Aleph*,"[1] or as "fundamental reading for the full understanding of his creative works."[2] They most certainly could be considered complementary to his narrative, but it is clear that they are a separate creative endeavor and should be studied accordingly. Yet we don't have critical work devoted to the essayist. A few explanations for such an anomaly can be suggested: (a) the overpowering success of his short stories, which have earned Borges the reputation he enjoys as a writer; (b) the misleading tendency, on the part of critics, to exclude the essays from his creative oeuvre; (c) the error of viewing the essay not as an entity in itself but rather as exegesis or supplement to poem or short story (an almost inevitable heresy when the essayist is also a poet and a short story writer); (d) the thin borderline between Borges' essay and short story and the consequent need to study one in conjunction with the other. Other reasons could be added. They might help to explain the void, but not to justify it. Just as Borges' short stories have been included in universal anthologies of this genre (*The Contemporary Short Story*, Columbia University Press), so his essays are now finding their way into similar collections. In the anthology entitled *50 Great Essays* (Bantam), next to the all-time masters of the genre, Borges is represented with four essays. There can be no doubt that Borges is as much a master of the essay as he is of the short story.

Borges has produced excellent studies on Lugones, Evaristo Carriego, and *Martín Fierro* by José Hernández. While his views and evaluations may be debatable, no serious student of Spanish American literature can overlook them—they represent definite contributions to criticism of the three poets' works. Yet it is not these lengthy essays (more than 60 pages) which lend full stature to Borges as an essayist. His contribution to the genre stems from the short essays collected in *Discusión* and *Otras inquisiciones* (Eng. tr., *Other Inquisitions*, 1964). The originality of these essays arises not from the manifold and erudite scope of their themes: the works of at least two well-established Latin American essayists—Alfonso Reyes and Ezequiel Martínez

Estrada—are equally as manifold and erudite. Reading the essays of Martínez Estrada and those of Borges, the reader immediately perceives a similar intention; both deny the efficacy of photographic realism and both mistrust Aristotelian logic. Speaking of Kafka, Martínez Estrada states: "he is not a writer of the fantastic except in respect to naive realism that accepts an order based on God, on reason, or on the logical happening of historical events. The world of the primitive has a greater functional resemblance to his. There, God is an inscrutable constellation; logic is a system of inferences based on observable analogies; and the organic process of events is filled with wonder, always open to the unforeseen. In short, a magic world . . ."[3] And Borges: "It is venturesome to think that a coordination of words (philosophies are nothing more than that) can resemble the universe very much" (*Labyrinths*, p. 207). And again: "A philosophical doctrine begins as a plausible description of the universe; as the years pass it becomes a mere chapter—if not a paragraph or a name—in the history of philosophy" (*Labyrinths*, p. 43). Like Borges, Martínez Estrada seeks to transcend an image of the world invented by "the deductive logic of Aristotle and Descartes" in order to draw near to a world which no longer can be categorized, a world perceived by intuition rather than thought by reason, a world closer to Lao Tzu than to Socratic Greece. But while Martínez Estrada seeks cognitive alternatives, because essentially he believes in the possibility of grasping "the true order of the world" (hence his enthusiasm for Kafka as a return to myth and the language of myth), Borges does not polarize Western reason and Oriental myth. He sees in Buddhism a form of idealism, and Schopenhauer—who had in his study a bust of Kant and a bronze Buddha—represents for Borges more than just a doctrine; it is a veritable reality or, as he puts it: "few things have happened to me more worth remembering than Schopenhauer's thought or the music of England's words" (*Dreamtigers*, p. 93). In opposition to Martínez Estrada's enthusiasm—an enthusiasm for a true order—Borges expresses a flat skepticism: if there is an order in the world, that order is not accessible to man. In both writers we find rejection of philosophical idealism, but in Borges this rejection is also a form of acceptance. Borges rejects the validity of philosophical idealism as an image or sketch of the world, but accepts its value as "a branch of fantastic literature." Borges' fiction is nurtured by the failure of philosophical theories or, as he says, by the "aesthetic worth [of those theories] and what is singular and marvelous about them" (*Other Inquisitions*, p. 201). By making them function as the coordinates of his short stories, Borges evinces their fallacy and their condition of being not "a mirror of the world, but rather [of] one thing more added to the world." Yet, despite differences (a transcendental faith in Martínez Estrada and a radical skepticism in Borges), in both authors the reader perceives a genuine effort to overcome the narrowness that Western tradition has imposed as master and measure of reality.

It is in the element of form that Borges' essay outweighs Martínez Estrada's. The essays of Estrada fall, with regard to form, within the rational orthodoxy they seek to refute. One might claim that such rationality is the distinctive mark of the essay, and that even when dealing with the most abstruse and least malleable of themes, the essayist is bound to elucidate in accordance with a system of reasoning that, in the final analysis, frames and defines the very essence of the essay. But it is precisely in this aspect that Borges offers an alternative. In his *Inquisitions* there is an imaginative dimension which is new to the Spanish American essay. Borges uses a technique similar to that of his fiction: the material of his essays is in some way subjected to metaphysical and theological ideas which make up, to a certain degree, our context of culture. Bearing this in mind one finds that his poems, short stories, and essays share certain constants which could be considered recurrent motifs or, as they have been called, Borgesian *topoi*. For example, the theme of order and chaos, basic to the short stories "The Library of Babel," "The Lottery in Babylonia," and "Tlön, Uqbar, Orbis Tertius," is set forth fully in the essay dedicated to "The Analytical Language of John Wilkins." The invention of John Wilkins receives precisely the same treatment as the short stories: "we do not know what the universe is. This world is perhaps the first rude essay of some infant deity who afterwards abandoned it, ashamed of his own performance . . . . But the impossibility of penetrating the divine scheme of the universe cannot dissuade us from outlining human schemes, even though we are aware that they are provisional. Wilkins's analytical language is not the least admirable of those schemes" (*Other Inquisitions*, p. 109). The same idea that forms the frame on which the stories are woven also constitutes the backbone of the essay: the analytical language of John Wilkins is just as powerless to penetrate reality as the efforts of the librarians to decipher the illegible books of the library of Babel. The analytical language of Wilkins and the ordered world of Tlön are both expressions of the same yearning for an order that is unattainable to human intelligence.

The *topos* of the universe as a dream or book of God, a central theme in the stories "The Circular Ruins," "The Dead Man," and "Death and the Compass," is also presented in all its perplexities in the essay "Forms of a Legend." Borges attempts to elucidate "the defects of logic" in the legend of Buddha, following an expositive order characteristic of many of his essays: (a) presentation of the subject or the question the essay intends to answer, (b) a summary of various theories which propound an explanation of the subject or an answer to the question (c) Borges' own solution, and (d) a conclusion, which generally dismisses both b and c as inevitably fallible. In c Borges explains that for the solution of the problem (the defects of logic in the legend) "It suffices to remember that all the religions of India and in particular Buddhism teach that the world is illusory. 'The minute narration of a game' [of a Buddha] is what Lalitavistara means . . . ; a game or a dream is, for Mahayana, the life of the Buddha on earth, which is another dream" (*Other Inquisitions*, pp. 160–61). Once again short story and essay share the same premise. This basic idea renders to the story a generic value that explains and intensifies the events of the fable, and to the essay a perspective that overcomes the "accidental errors" and converts them into "substantial truth." Even in a short story so apparently close to the realistic model as "Emma Zunz," Borges interprets the events of the narration by the same principle. In the last paragraph he says: "Actually, the story *was* incredible, but it impressed everyone because substantially it was true" (*Labyrinths*, p. 137). In the essay he asserts: "The chronology of India is uncertain; my erudition is even more unreliable. Koeppen and Hermann Beckh are perhaps as fallible as the compiler who has hazarded this article. It would not surprise me if my story of the legend turned out to be legendary, formed of substantial truth and accidental errors" (*Other Inquisitions*, p. 162). The "accidental errors" of the essay and the "false circumstances" of the short story represent the contingent immediacy of reality, the limits of a province where Aristotelian logic prevails. In the essay as well as in the short story Borges attempts to cross these logical limits to explore a reality that can no longer be translated into facile syllogisms, because the postulates of the essay are erroneous, yet true, and the events of the story of Emma Zunz are false, but substantially true.

Numerous examples of this correlation between the essay and the short story could be cited. But since the real concern here is to define Borges' contribution to the essay, the above examples will have to suffice. What Martínez Estrada suggests for a more thorough understanding of Kafka's message will also help us, to a certain extent, to define the mechanics of Borges' essays. In the one on "Literal Meaning of Myth in Kafka" the author of *Radiografía de la Pampa* observes that "in order to understand Kafka's message, his stupendous revelation of a reality previously glimpsed only in flashes, it must be recognized that all that truly occurs does so in conformity with the language of myth, because it is pure myth (mathematics is also a mythical system). Therefore the most meaningful way of expressing that reality is through its logical connotation, that is: myth and allegory."[4] Martínez Estrada understands myth as "a logical system of better understanding the inexpressible."[5] In the case of Kafka, myth represents a form of "not accepting the hideous and conventional order of a reality conditioned by norm and factitious law."[6] We previously stated that in both essay and short story Borges draws upon metaphysics and theology. These two disciplines make up, in essence, the antithesis of myth: the first attempts to substitute myth with reason; the second, exorcism with doctrine. To attribute to Borges, then, the use of myth would be an obvious contradiction. It is not so, though, if we recall his tendency "to evaluate religious or philosophical ideas on the basis of their aesthetic worth and even for what is singular and marvelous about them" (*Other Inquisitions*, p. 201). Thus Borges reduces philosophical and theological ideas to mere creations of the imagination, to intuitions that differ little from any other mythical form. This modus operandi brings several of his narratives to mind: a two or three centimeter disc that encompasses the universe in "The Zahir"; Averroes defining the Greek words "comedy" and "tragedy" without ever knowing what a theater was; a library of undecipherable books; Pierre Menard composing *Don Quijote* in the twentieth century; a pursuer being pursued in "Death and the Compass." This oxymoronic treatment is found with equal success in Borges' essays. Having reduced the products of philosophy and theology to myths, there is no reason not to perform the same operation with other phenomena of culture. Thus the myths of intelligence would be restored to the only reality that befits them: not to the labyrinth created by the gods but to the labyrinth invented by man. Borges approaches cultural values to understand them not in the context of reality but in the only context open to man—his own created culture. John Donne's "Biathanatos" is understood according to the law of causality. The essays "Pascal's Sphere" and "The Flower of Coleridge" are examples which show that "perhaps universal history is the history of the diverse intonation of a few metaphors" (*Other Inquisitions*, p. 8). And the avatars of Zeno's tortoise, as well as the solutions of Aristotle, Agrippa, St. Thomas, Bradley, William James, Descartes, Leibniz, Bergson, Bertrand Russell, and others, are explained in the lapidary phrase: "the world is a fabrication of the will" (*Other Inquisitions*, p. 120), a paraphrase from a book so dear to Borges, *The World as Will and Idea*.[7] The enigma of Omar Khayyám's *Rubáiyát* and the later Fitzgerald version is resolved with the assistance of a pantheistic concept: "the Englishman could have recreated the Persian, because both were, essentially, God—or momentary faces of God" (*Other Inquisitions*, p. 82). A similar solution is applied to the problem of Kubla Khan—a palace built by a thirteenth-century Mongolian emperor in a dream related in Samuel Coleridge's poem of the same name—with Borges' essay "The Dream of Coleridge."

Thus, treatment of themes in the essays does not differ, basically, from that employed in the narrations. There are some instances in which the short story is merely a variation or an elaboration of material contained in the essay, as exemplified in "The Library of Babel" with regard to "The Total Library" (essay). This first conclusion reveals in itself the outlook of culture manifest in the Borgesian essay: the various expressions of the human spirit with which his essays deal are understood not as attempts to comprehend or interpret the historical universe, but rather as schemes of a world "constructed by means of logic, with little or no appeal to concrete experience."[8] In essence, this prognosis is the same as that posited by Martínez Estrada for the study of Kafka: "reason first shaped the world, and then enjoyed understanding and explaining it rationally . . . ."[9] The originality of Borges, then, does not lie in the premise. He has coined one of the most ingenious and fertile formulations of it—"the impossibility of penetrating the divine scheme of the universe cannot dissuade us from outlining human schemes, even though we are aware that they are provisional" (*Other Inquisitions*, p. 109), or "metaphysics is a branch of fantastic literature"—but he is far from being the first to express such disbelief. Already Kant, "half seriously and half in jest, suggested that Swedenborg's mystical system, which he calls 'fantastic,' is perhaps no more so than orthodox metaphysics."[10] Levi-Strauss has shown that history as we read it in books has little to do with reality; he later explains that "the historian and the agent of history choose, sever and carve the historical facts, for a truly total history would confront them with chaos, and so 'the French Revolution,' as it is known, never took place."[11] Mathematicians tell us that "the characteristic of mathematical thought is that it does not convey truth about the external world."[12] But the reference that bears closest affinity to Borges' spirit of the metaphor, and also the closest in formulation, is a paragraph from Cassirer's essay *Language and Myth*, which we quote:

> Consequently all schemata which science evolves in order to classify, organize, and summarize the phenomena of the real world turn out to be nothing but arbitrary schemes—airy fabrics of the mind, which express not the nature of things, but the

nature of mind. So knowledge, as well as myth, language, and art, has been reduced to a kind of fiction—to a fiction that recommends itself by its usefulness, but must not be measured by any strict standard of truth, if it is not to melt away into nothingness.[13]

Why not make fiction out of theories and doctrines that are fictional anyhow? Borges seems to have himself persuaded that "Parmenides, Plato, John Scotus Erigena, Spinoza, Leibniz, Kant, and Francis Bradley are the unsuspected and greatest masters of fantastic literature" (*Discusión*, p. 172). The themes of his stories are often inspired in metaphysical hypotheses accumulated through many centuries of the history of philosophy, and in theological systems that are the scaffoldings of several religions. His originality stems from the creative use of this material in his narratives, as much as in his essays. The results in the latter are no less fruitful than in the former. With Borges the essay attains a new quality in which structure becomes an effective expressive vehicle for the intended theme. As with the oxymoron, where a word is modified by an epithet which seems to contradict it, in his essays Borges studies a subject by applying theories that he has previously condemned as fallible and fallacious. Oxymoron is an attempt to overcome the inherent narrowness that reason has imposed on language; it is a "no" to a reality conceptually ruled by words. This stylistic device best defines the technique of Borges' essay because the ideas being dealt with are evaluated or modified by theories which contradict those ideas, stripping them of all transcendent value in historical reality.[14] At the same time those theories function as oxymoronic modifiers in a different way—they restore the ideas, the subject matter of the essay, to a level where they regain their validity, not as a description of the world but as marvels of human imagination. Thus the seeming contradiction between the two terms (a theory acting as modifier and an idea standing as a noun) is in essence a form of conciliation. The incongruity, then, is only illusory. The two components of the oxymoron clash on a conventional level only to reach a deeper and richer level of reality. Like any other literary trope, it represents an effort to correct through language the deficiencies of language itself. The oxymoronic structure of Borges' essay is likewise an attempt to bring theories and ideas to a plane where their shortcomings find an adequate corrective within the realm of those same theories and ideas. The two terms may often seem to contradict each other. It is only so because we insist on seeing them in the context of reality, where they no longer belong. In their new context—human imagination and fantasy—Borges establishes a new set of values by means of which metaphysics and theology, and for that matter any product of the human mind, is no less fantastic than, say, the Ptolemaic system. Hence Borges' assertion with reference to Donne's theory of time: "With such a splendid thesis as that, any fallacy committed by the author becomes insignificant" (*Other Inquisitions*, p. 21).

Borges' essays would not have reached their high degree of originality if he had merely followed the discursive patterns of structure traditionally accepted in the essay form. Martínez Estrada saw in Kafka and in myth in general the use of magic to perceive a magical world. Borges has renounced that possibility with respect to the world but not with respect to intellectual culture. He has given up the labyrinth of the gods but not the labyrinth of man.[15] His way of perceiving this human labyrinth is based on illustrious ideas: cyclical time, pantheism, the law of causality, the world as dream or idea, and some others. But for Borges they are no longer absolute truths, as once claimed, but marvels, intuitions, myths. Myths by which man attempts to understand not that magic reality unattainable for feeble human intelligence, but rather that other reality woven by laborious undertakings and painstaking endeavors of the human mind in an effort to penetrate the impenetrable. In spite of their rational nature they are myths, because they function in the essay for the creation of oxymoronic relationships that not only challenge traditional order, but open the possibility of a completely new understanding of the subject. According to this understanding, man has been denied access to the world. He is confronted with the only alternative left at his disposal: to sublimate his impotence toward reality by creating another reality; and this man-made reality is the only one accessible to man. One could indeed say, with Borges the world has become Tlön. The poet "makes or invents himself in his poetry," according to Octavio Paz; the writer, in Borges' own words, "sets himself the task of portraying the world . . ., to discover, shortly before his death, that that patient labyrinth of lines traces the image of his face" (*Dreamtigers*, p. 93). Man, powerless to know the world, has invented through the products of culture his own image of the world. Thus he lives in a reality designed by his own fragile architecture. He knows that there is another "irreversible and iron-clad" reality which constantly besieges him and forces him to feel the enormousness of its presence, and between these two realities, between these two dreams, between these two stories (one imagined by god and another invented by man) flows the painfully-sore history of humanity. There is a moment in Borges' essay in which he captures this tragic condition of man in a memorable sentence which epitomizes man's plight as both dream and dreamer; it occurs at the end of "A New Refutation of Time," one of his most remarkable essays: "The world, unfortunately, is real; I, unfortunately, am Borges."

University of California, San Diego

Translated from the Spanish by Thomas E. Lyon

---

[1] James Irby, Introduction to *Other Inquisitions*, New York, 1965, p. vii.

[2] Emir Rodríguez Monegal, "Borges, essayiste," *L'Herne*, Paris, 1964, p. 345.

[3] Ezequiel Martínez Estrada, *En torno a Kafka y otros ensayos*, Barcelona, 1967, p. 30.

[4] *Ibid.*, p. 35.

[5] *Ibid.*, p. 34.

[6] *Ibid.*

[7] For a more detailed discussion of Borges' contacts with Schopenhauer see notes 13 (chapter I) and 9 (chapter VI) of my study, *La prosa narrativa de J. L. Borges*, Madrid, 1968, pp. 29–30, 82.

[8] Bertrand Russell, *Our Knowledge of the External World*, New York, 1960, p. 15.

[9] Martínez Estrada, p. 24.

[10] Bertrand Russell, *A History of Western Philos-* ophy, New York, 1965, pp. 705–706.

[11] Claude Levi-Strauss, *The Savage Mind*, Chicago, 1966, p. 258.

[12] *Ibid.*, p. 248.

[13] Ernest Cassirer, *Language and Myth*, New York, 1946, pp. 7–8.

[14] On the use of oxymoron in Borges' style see the chapter "Adjetivación" in my *La prosa narrativa de J. L. Borges*, pp. 186–95.

[15] The reference is to a widely quoted passage from the story "Tlön, Uqbar, Orbis Tertius." There Borges says: "It is useless to answer that reality is also orderly. Perhaps it is, but in accordance with divine laws—I translate: inhuman laws—which we never quite grasp. Tlön is surely a labyrinth, but it is a labyrinth devised by men, a labyrinth destined to be deciphered by men" (*Labyrinths*, pp. 17–18).

The Visible Work
of Macedonio Fernández

By JOHN C. MURCHISON

Macedonio Fernández, who died in Buenos Aires in 1952, remains unknown to most people, and an enigma to a few. That is what he would have wished. But his influence on Jorge Luis Borges was decisive, and it is our purpose here to find out why, even at the risk of dusting off his memory. To those who knew him, he survives simply as "Macedonio": the unassuming family name, which had long ago paled before that trenchant title, was further whittled away by friendship, by friends.

For thirty years Jorge Luis Borges was fortunate in being the friend of Macedonio, a man to whom friendship was a passion and a deep joy. A friend and a disciple, Borges frankly and quite proudly admits that "during those years I imitated him to the point of copying, to the point of passionate and devoted plagiarism . . . . Not to have imitated his work would have amounted to an unbelievable oversight."[1]

But the imitation of Macedonio was a constant, vital, and by no means merely literary process, since for Borges all art is an intimate part of life and not to be separated. It could be that one of the lessons of this master, this Argentine *Zaddik*, was precisely that idea. Macedonio's secret skill, the one he practiced best, was to teach the people around him not only to think, but to regard life itself as intense and constant thought. If Macedonio's literary production is limited in bulk and remains obscure, his other art, the invisible one, has borne remarkable fruit in Borges.

Very little can be told of Macedonio's life by someone who did not know him to others who likewise did not know him. He was born in Buenos Aires in 1874; as a young men he went to live in the forests of Paraguay, in the role of a utopian anarchist. Later, as District Attorney for the Province of Misiones, he was fired for never bringing anyone to trial. He was also, for years, a vague sort of lawyer, and at one point he corresponded with William James. But these few facts belong to what one of his friends, Fernández Latour, described as Macedonio's "prehistory." His true existence began around 1923 or 1924, at a homage for the painter Pedro Figari. The occasion marked his public debut as a speaker—to a notoriously reduced audience which was, in fact, not much larger than his own circle of immediate friends. Among these were Borges' father, Jorge Guillermo, and Borges himself, who, on his return from Europe a couple of years earlier, had inherited that friendship. Precisely that friendship, and the meaning it held for Macedonio, concern us here, for these things hold the key to understanding his life and the influence he had on others.

It is difficult to capture, through time gone by, and from so great a distance, the intangible essence of that sense of friendship. Perhaps because Buenos Aires is a city of exorbitant size, of extravagant crowds, Macedonio thought that the closeness and intimacy of a few offered a sort of respite or salvation from the disquieting enormity which, ironically, somehow repeats the vastness of the surrounding pampa. Perhaps because in that "feast of clarity," as Ramón Gómez de la Serna called Buenos Aires at the time, Macedonio felt he was not understood he searched for the solace offered by those few who admired him. The fact remains that he lived for his friends, for the joy of sharing with them—as others with equal ardor give themselves to medicine or high finance—what Borges has called "the quiet adventure of conversation." Macedonio made friendship into a career, a devotedly held vocation. In fact, his life was ruled by friendship; on that basis, everything else was bound to be diminished. His career as a writer, for example, seems frustrated, since only a few of Macedonio's works have been published and then in editions which are as modest as they are careless. But to Macedonio, publication was a form of vanity, and anyway, he was too busy being a friend. Besides, Macedonio felt that writing need be no more than a rough draft, a sketchy and impoverished version of his thought. With this idea in mind, writing came almost too easily:

> Writing was no great task for Macedonio . . . . He lived . . . in order to think. Daily he would give himself over to the vicissitudes and the surprises of reasoning . . . and that manner of reasoning which is called writing cost him not the slightest effort. His thought was as vivid as its translation onto paper; alone in his room, or in a bustling café, he would fill page after page . . . .[2]

The written reproduction of thought was the principal task, not its laborious literary distillation. He felt, for instance, "an incorrigible dislike for verbal sonorities and even for euphony. 'I don't go for pretty patter,' he once declared, and the prosodic anxieties undergone by Lugones or Darío seemed to him completely worthless."[3]

This is not to say that Macedonio was not concerned with aesthetics. On the contrary, the subject held singular interest for him, but it was the philosopher's interest more than the artist's. Throughout his work, even if unmethodically set down, Macedonio takes a stand with regard to aesthetic pleasure. This stand bears scrutiny, since it will give us the clue not only to his thought, but also to the relationship between the latter and the life of a man whom Borges himself has defined as first a philosopher, then a poet and novelist.

As we have seen, Macedonio didn't "go for pretty patter." He sought music in music, not in language. This was because language to Macedonio was only a more or less successful method for transmitting an emotion to the reader. Supposing a division between prose and poetry, Macedonio preferred the former; but, of course, not all prose was artistic or held aesthetic value. Prose which did meet those aims received the distinction of being known as "*belarte*." And "*belarte*," for Macedonio, is only to be found when words are able to produce in the reader "states of being entirely exempt from *notion*"[4] that is, when words are able to call forth only an emotional response. More precisely, what Macedonio seeks is *incitación* in the sense Ortega uses the word, that of a primary emotional response translated into thought in order to become action.

In accordance with this theory, the novel rather than the essay was Macedonio's favorite prose genre. The essay is primarily involved with getting ideas across. The novel, on the other hand, allows and supposes interplay between the life and feelings of the characters and of the reader; the flux is dynamic and emotional rather than static and intellectual.

Obviously, Macedonio's creed is based on the reader, who is to participate, ideally, in the fusion and identification of art and life. The novel, therefore, says Macedonio, "aspires to create in the psyche of the reader 'the moment of abolition of the conscious being, using the characters . . . to make the reader, if only for an instant, believe himself to *be* a character, snatched from life,' and thereby achieving 'the substitution of the vital happening of the reader by that of the character' . . . ."[5]

The corollary to this function of the novel is that of intellectual shock or surprise, achieved through humor. A conceptual and essentially Spanish humor runs in Macedonio like a calm reaffirmation of his roots, a flowering of Quevedo in Buenos Aires: "the great basis for pleasure in what is amusing or comical is hedonism, established on a candid slice of life (realistic amusement) or on a forceful mental impossibility (conceptual amusement). Conceptual amusement . . . is that which true humor requires."[6] And later, in *Papeles de Reciénvenido* (The Newcomer Papers), he would define the joke thus:

> . . . there are many people who experience pleasure (emotional), each time they become aware of an action, situation, aptitude or condition of pleasure or happiness either present or probable, or conducive to pleasure or well-being, in another person . . . when this pleasure (sympathetic) is motivated by an unexpected event, or when the contrary was foreseen or feared (someone else's discomfort) that pleasure is released in laughter . . . .[7]

And, ideally, that "forceful mental impossibility" is what "deprives the reader . . . momentarily, of his intellect . . . it consists of thrusting the reader towards a transitory belief in the absurd, soon to be replaced by the return to normal consciousness."[8]

Here, as always, and prior to any other consideration, is Macedonio's concern for the reader made evident; that concern is the point of departure between Macedonio's affectionate brand of humor and Quevedo's harsh and biting wit. Quevedo writes for and against the populace. Macedonio, perhaps more oppressed by it than the Master of Torre Abad, chooses to ignore it and write solely for his friends. This is not a case of purposefully writing for the few, of being consciously "elitist"; Macedonio is generously and sincerely willing to believe that intelligence and sensitivity are a common patrimony. Nevertheless, these theories, when translated into practice, admittedly achieve only partial success. The theoretical emphasis on the reader is so strong that it overwhelms everything else in his literary work. Macedonio manages his characters with the reader in mind in order to allow the reader, momentarily at least, to feel himself a character, but his technique eliminates *a priori* the chance of creating great literary characters. Miss Eternal, Sweet-Person, Neargenius, Ofalove, in "Museum of the Novel of Miss Eternal" all perform the steps dictated to them by the expert in narrative technique and criticism. We witness their development; we overhear their conversations with the author-narrator. But we never feel they live; their actions are not free but preordained.

Of course, that which may be a failure from the point of view of the literary critic is not necessarily so for the author. On the contrary, Macedonio believed that literary success would entail the true failure of his intentions, and declares as much in the aforementioned work:

> There is one kind of reader with whom I hold constant quarrel: the kind who seeks what all novelists, to their own discredit, have sought, what they give this kind of reader: Hallucination. I want the reader to be aware all the time that he is reading a novel, and not seeing a life, not facing 'life' itself. As soon as the reader falls into Hallucination, Art's ignominy, I have lost, not gained, him. What I want is very difficult; it is to gain him as a character, that is to say, to make him believe for a moment that he is not alive. This is the feeling he must thank me for, the feeling nobody has ever thought of giving him.[9]

From this one might gather that Macedonio was basically misanthropic. Nothing, however, could be further from the the truth. On the contrary, as Borges has pointed out, Macedonio was terrified of death; a terror he was barely able to overcome by the methodical denial of self. And since he lived with that great fear, it followed that others, his friends, must also live with it. Macedonio felt that to awaken them to the possibility of not-living while alive would somehow lessen the fear of death, since it is only possible to feel the notion of not-living, or non-being, while alive. He writes that

> this impression, never made through the written word to anyone, this impression that I would like to inaugurate with my novel in human psychology . . . is a blessing for all consciences, since it obliterates the felt or intellective fear which we call fear of not-being, and so, liberates us from it. Whoever experiments for a moment the state of belief in non-existence, and then returns to the state of belief in existence, will realize forevermore that the entire content of the wording or feeling of 'non-existence' is the belief in not being."[10]

From the notion that characters in a novel must have no life—we may recall the desperate attempts of Maybe-genius and Sweet-Person in "Museum"—together with the notion that to write a novel is to try to make the reader feel himself a character in it (and thus, to be conscious of the blessed state of non-being), Macedonio derived another idea for a novel—which never progressed beyond the first couple of chapters—and which, precisely because of that fact and its unexpected corollary, constitutes his greatest success and the justification for his efforts as artist and philosopher.

That novel began in Buenos Aires; it is still unfinished; it continues today, perhaps with myself, perhaps with all of us. Borges recalls how Macedonio at one moment "played with the vast if vague project of becoming President of the Republic,"[11] and for that purpose enlisted the help of his friends. They were charged, for example, with leaving on streetcars, in movie houses, and in bars small cards that carried nothing but the mysterious word "Macedonio." Thus, according to Macedonio, he would subtly insinuate himself into the collective consciousness of the people. Let us listen to one of the characters of this great fantastic novel speak, in the best tradition of narrative trickery, of the novel's inception:

> From these more or less imaginary manouvres . . . arose the project of a great fantastic novel, placed in Buenos Aires, and which we began to write among us . . . the work was titled "The Man Who Would be President"; the characters were Macedonio's friends, and on the last page the reader would come across the revelation that the book had been written by Macedonio Fernández, the hero . . . and by Jorge Luis Borges, who killed himself towards the end of Chapter Nine, and by Carlos Pérez Ruiz, who had that singular adventure with the rainbow, and so forth . . . . We wanted . . . the style to grow as mad as the events; we chose for the first chapter the chatty tone of Pío Baroja; the last chapter would have been equal to the most baroque pages of Quevedo . . . . In this unfinished novel there may well be some involuntary glimmerings of *The Man Who Was Thursday*.[12]

The reader has probably guessed by now to whom this extensive quote belongs. Borges himself is the character, caught forever within the net wrought by Macedonio's friendship; wrought by Macedonio to make art an ally of life, helping life to go on forever; wrought by Macedonio so that Borges, whenever he should recall that "vast and vague project," would feel the web of affection woven by his friend. And Borges, speaking of Macedonio, speaking of the "unfinished novel," is well within the narrative techniques which were well-known by Macedonio and which laboriously appear in his other works, serving thus as an introduction to the great work of art in which Borges himself partakes, so that, affirming the great project with his very presence, he *is* "the *visible* work of Macedonio Fernández."

Also, as a literary character Borges necessarily had to feel the influence of the author's ideas, and truly Macedonio found in Borges an avid disciple. During those first dazzling years of their friendship, Borges was able to think that the very fact of seeing Macedonio once a week, hearing him transform reality from prosaic to astonishing, compensated amply for all of Europe:

> I spoke a couple of times with Macedonio, and I understood that this grey man, who, in a mediocre rooming-house . . . was rediscovering the eternal problems as if he were Thales or Parmenides, could replace infinitely the cities and kingdoms of Europe . . . the sure knowledge that on Saturday, in a coffee-house in the Once, we would be hearing Macedonio explain what sort of absence or illusion is the self, was enough, I remember vividly, to justify the entire week. In the course of a life already lengthy, there has been no dialogue which impressed me as much as Macedonio Fernández' . . . .[13]

And in that coffee-house where Macedonio's friends would gather to listen to Macedonio—who hardly spoke, who would, instead, slip in a query now and then—Borges recalls him thus: "beyond the charm of his dialogue and the reserved presence of his friendship, Macedonio was proposing his example of an intellectual way of life."[14] Of life and thought, since both activities went together and were akin if not synonymous for Macedonio. Life as thought, as a high adventure of the intellect: this could well be the main gift Macedonio bestowed on Borges. And since the identification between life and thought inevitably must touch upon idealism, it is no surprise that Borges, an apt disciple, drawn already to the surprises and paradoxes which adorn idealistic systems, should allow Macedonio to confirm him in his ways.

It was this outlook on life, this vital point of view, more than a given literary style, which had singular influence on Borges. An ascetic in search of pure ideas and absolute truth, Macedonio approaches mysticism when he considers that truth, even if easily accessible given the proper circumstances, may well be both ineffable and incommunicable, and only capable of being alluded to indirectly. Thus a certain skepticism toward the word, a chancy tool in the best of cases, and the idea that to perpetuate the word through print is proof of vanity. Ideas, not their imprecise verbal reproduction, are the essence, and Macedonio, typically, was a great speaker not because he spoke a great deal, but rather because what little he said carried with it the magical power of the idea which at once enriches and transforms reality.

This Socratic method of inquiry was inevitably to have disastrous effects on literature, if the latter is to be considered as the expression of a desire to endure through the written word. Macedonio mistrusted literature as a valid or even worthy enterprise: his antiheros, his particular nemesis, were precisely those writers who raised the written work to the level of both means and end in itself—the jewellers of words, those who exhibited and caressed them as rare gems. Thus, for example, he much admired Mark Twain, whom he physically resembled, but felt uncomfortable with Valéry.

Borges, by nature more inclined to revere literature and the art and livelihood of writing, still came under the influence of Macedonio's skepticism. Convinced, as was Macedonio, that a writer deals with only a few ideas whose variations and repetitions constitute the main thrust of the written work, Borges prefers the succinct exposition to furbelows and verbal fireworks. His oft-mentioned laziness is only partly Argentine. It corresponds to a metaphysical system which leads him to mistrust extension and to rely on the almost epigrammatic brevity which is a hallmark of his style.

This is not to say that Macedonio's literary style is similar to that of Borges, even though the latter has come to think so. On the contrary, there is an abyss separating the two as far as literary quality is concerned. Macedonio is the kind of writer who reaps fatigue from the constant and conscientious reader. The whirlwind of witticisms, each chained to the preceding in a causal relationship, destroys the logic nexus of the whole and dulls, indeed stupefies, the reader. It is a febrile, enervating, hothouse style. Borges, the "man of letters," capable of seeing that effect, affectionately strives to save his friend's reputation by presenting us with the finest anthology of Macedonio Fernández available, since the anthology—so Borges believes—has the virtue of improving the writer by showing only his best side, in brief selections palatable to the reader.

If it is true that there are great differences between the styles of the two writers, it is also certain that the narrative techniques of both are curiously alike. One could define Macedonio as a writer who reveals himself through the very act of writing: we may recall, for instance, the comically interminable series of prefaces to the "Museum," prefaces which nevertheless constitute an integral and instructive part of the problem of the novel. A skeptical lesson, the book arrives fatally at the conclusion that the novel as a literary genre has seen its halcyon days: the new novel is that one which will mingle fully with life, and thus will not rely on the written word, not on the page, but on memory, on the temporal flow of the characters themselves, as is the case of "The Man Who Would Be President."

In Borges, the notion of the author writing on the problems of writing itself is also prevalent: "The Secret Miracle" is a mystic parable of the quandary of the writer face to face with Time. "The Aleph" ponders the problem, indeed the possibility, of expression. But where this skeptical approach to literature is most manifest, in a most subtle way, is in "Three Versions of Judas." There, woven into the plot of the sophistical heresies of Nils Runeberg, is the other argument, whose disillusioned hero is Borges himself: the "runes" of the heretic theologian's surname give us, almost in jest, the clue of the "berg," the "burgh," the Borges who hides within the cryptic message of the Viking lance. The story, which depicts Runeberg claiming that his own obscurity is a part of God's plan, becomes a commentary on the condition and fate of the writer of the tale.

In short, through similar structural devices we find a similar, probably inherited, skeptical attitude toward life and letters. Macedonio's influence on Borges was vitally pervasive, not merely literary, and it was due to Macedonio's rare gift for being both friend and master. With him, his disciples shared a rejoicing in friendship, fostered by a common outlook and vision. Borges had the good fortune to know and the genius to appreciate Macedonio, in his precise measure, and to cherish this friend among friends.

In the case of another famous friend of friends, Federico García Lorca, the poet was able to lament his lost friend, the bullfighter Ignacio Sánchez Mejías, with words we now feel define the singer himself: "Tardará mucho tiempo en nacer, si es que nace,/un andaluz tan claro, tan rico de aventura. . . ."[15] This transferral is born out of the total mutual penetration of a truly great friendship. Borges, speaking in his turn of his own lost friend, recoverable only in memory, in the "affectionate mythology" of those who survive Macedonio, reaches with equal lyricism, all unknowing, his own definition:

> The best possibilities of that which is Argentine—lucidity, modesty, courtesy, intimate passion, and genial friendship—were realized in Macedonio, perhaps more fully than in other, more famous contemporaries.[16]

Tufts University

[1] Jorge Luis Borges, "Macedonio Fernández," *Sur* March-April 1952, p. 146.

[2] ———, *Macedonio Fernández*, Ediciones Culturales Argentinas, Buenos Aires, 1961, p. 15.

[3] *Ibid.*, pp. 15–16.

[4] César Fernández Moreno, *Introducción a Macedonio Fernández*, Ediciones Talía, Buenos Aires, 1960, p. 17.

[5] *Ibid.*

[6] *Ibid.*

[7] *Ibid.*

[8] *Ibid.*, pp. 18–19.

[9] Macedonio Fernández, *Papeles de Reciénvenido*, Losada, Buenos Aires, 1944, p. 183.

[10] ———, *Museo de la novela de la Eterna*, Centro Ed. de la América Latina, Buenos Aires, 1967, p. 39.

[11] Borges, *Macedonio Fernández*, p. 17.

[12] Borges, *Sur*, p. 146.

[13] *Ibid.*, p. 146.

[14] *Ibid.*

[15] Federico García Lorca, "Llanto por Ignacio Sánchez Mejías," in *Obras Completas*, Aguilar, Madrid, 1960, p. 473.

[16] Borges, *Sur*, p. 146.

Borges and Lowell Dunham, University of Oklahoma, December, 1969.

Borges and Norman Thomas di Giovanni, December, 1969.

At Work with Borges

By NORMAN THOMAS DI GIOVANNI

I.

Borges and I first met for the purpose of working together on the translation of a volume of his poetry. I had written him a letter about the project, and he had asked me to pay him a visit. That was in December 1967, while he was at Harvard. I paid the visit and, like the man who came to dinner, never left. We liked each other, we enjoyed the work, and it was the right hour to have come knocking. At the time, Borges was suffering from an unhappy marriage and from the peculiar isolation it had created. I had happened along, all unwittingly, to help fill those long empty Sundays he so dreaded, to offer him the kind of work he could yield his mind to (this in turn earned him much needed self-justification), and to lend him the ear he desperately needed. It was a lucky chain of events, and it kept getting luckier. Three different foundations flocked to support the expensive work of putting together the book of poems. The Poetry Center of the YM-YWHA asked us to organize a Borges reading in New York. Magazines began taking notice of what we were doing; and when we experimented collaborating on the translation of one of his stories, the *New Yorker* magazine not only took it but offered us a contract for all of Borges' untranslated works, past and future. The next April, before we parted, Borges invited me to Buenos Aires and gave me carte blanche to handle all his publishing affairs in English. In the course of those five months, we had done enough and been through enough to forge a friendship.

For the past two years I have been living in Buenos Aires, where Borges and I are producing English versions of eleven of his books—ten of them for E. P. Dutton and one for Seymour Lawrence. Of these, *The Book of Imaginary Beings* was published in 1969, *The Aleph and Other Stories* in 1970; two titles are scheduled for 1971, and four others are in progress. In this same two-year period, while Borges has written new collections of poems and stories, I have accompanied him on lecture trips, we have given poetry readings, we have composed a long essay on his life, and we have compiled comments on his *Aleph* stories. Further travels are planned, further work is projected, and I think I may safely predict that a great deal more amusement and satisfaction lie in store for us. All told, our nine remaining translations embrace three volumes of essays, two of poems, and four of prose fiction.

In this essay I want to discuss briefly our method of translation and our aims, and then, taking examples from a recent work, go into detail about problems and their solutions. I shall not discuss the poetry translations or the translations we are making, with Adolfo Bioy Casares, of the Bustos Domecq sketches written by Bioy and Borges in collaboration; I have already touched on the subject of translating Borges' poetry elsewhere, and the work we are doing with Bioy is really the topic for another discussion. In the course of my remarks, I want to give some idea of what it is like to be in daily association with Borges.

II.

At the outset, working alone, I make a handwritten rough draft of whatever story, essay, or piece we choose to translate. I bring this to Borges. We work every afternoon and occasionally on Saturday mornings at the Biblioteca Nacional; we have also worked at his apartment, at mine, and in any number of *confiterías* in downtown Buenos Aires. First I read him a sentence of the Spanish text and afterward a sentence of my draft. Sometimes we feel these sentences are good enough as they stand, and sometimes we revise them extensively. Borges may correct me; I may ask him to clarify; one or the other of us may suggest alternatives or variations. To keep sentences free of cumbersome or indirect constructions, we both make constant efforts to rephrase. Many times, as soon as the draft sentence comes off my tongue, we pounce on it together, seeing immediately how it can be made better. But our underlying concern at this point is to get all the Spanish into some kind of English, and in order to do this I like to be sure I have a complete understanding not only of the text but also of Borges' intentions. Therefore, as this stage approaches completion, we are not troubled by the fact that in any given place we may still be fairly literal and makeshift. Many times, in fact, we remain purposely undecided about such details as finding the right word or choosing between various alternatives.

Then the second stage begins. I take the draft home, type it out, and go to work shaping and polishing the sentences and paragraphs by supplying exact words. Any reference I make back to the Spanish text at this juncture is usually for checking rhythms and emphases only. My preoccupations now are almost exclusively with matters of tone, tension, and style. The big worry here is over timing and effects. These are not translation problems; they are writing problems. A number of cases come to mind where I have had to sit for an hour or so putting together and taking apart the difficult opening sentence of a Borges story, testing various balances and rhythms, and sounding it over and over before hitting upon a solution. This, of course, is the hardest stage of the work, the aim being to cast the piece in the best possible English style.

During the final stage, I bring the new draft, which I consider more or less finished, back to Borges. I read it to him, this time without any reference whatsoever to the original Spanish. He never fails to recommend (echoing Swinburne), "Fling it aside and be free!" The work has no other existence for us now; at this point our sole aim is to see that the piece reads as though it were written in English. Small adjustments are made—a word changed here and there, sometimes a phrase altered. Occasionally Borges will add a sentence or a bit of dialogue or make an emendation that did not occur to him while he wrote the Spanish. We usually translate this dictated material from English into Spanish for insertion into the original text—if it is unpublished. If the work is already in print, we supply his publisher with a list of changes for future editions. Then we are finished. The piece is freshly typed and signed as having been translated "in collaboration with the author." Borges tells me this is the first time he has ever taken a direct hand in any translation of his own work.

Underlying this method, obviously, are a lot of tacit assumptions, agreements, and other interlocking factors that guide what we do and how we do it. Principally, on Borges' side, are his command of English, his sense of English prose style, what amounts almost to a preference for the English language over his own; and his seemingly inexhaustible powers of invention; also, the good clear writing; the carefully constructed, balanced, and rhythmic sentences that are written with the ear and largely modeled on English sentence structure; and the restraint, that absence of rhetoric which is so un-Spanish and so much the hallmark of the quiet prose so admired in the best English language writing. Then too, there is Borges' advanced blindness, which makes it impossible for him to read—even this works to our advantage, because having to communicate orally every word (and sometimes the punctuation as well) is built-in insurance against scamping. At the same time, in sounding our sentences aloud we continually test them for effect and readability.

In addition to the foregoing elements, Borges and I hold in common a whole groundwork of ideas—which, naturally, become our own personal rules—about what makes a good translation and what, specifically, makes a good English translation from the Spanish. We agree, for example, that a translation should not sound like a translation. We agree that words having Anglo-Saxon roots are preferable to words of Latin origin—or, to put it another way, that the first English word suggested by the Spanish should usually be avoided (for instance, for "*solitario*," not "solitary" but "lonely"; for "*rígido*," not "rigid" but "stiff"; or, taking an illustration Borges likes to use, not "obscure habitation" but "dark room"). We agree also that the text should not be approached as a sacred object but as a tool, allowing us, whenever we feel the need, to add or subtract from it, to depart from it, or even, on rare occasions, to improve it. We make these changes recognizing, of course, that the reader for whom Borges writes and the reader for whom we translate are entirely different persons.

On my own side, through residence in Argentina, daily contact with Borges, and complete dedication to the work, I am able to bring to our translations a wealth of background knowledge and preparation otherwise not easy to come by. (Furthermore —luxury of luxuries—because our work is well paid, I am free to lavish all the time I like on each piece we produce.) I cannot stress this personal association enough, for no matter what we do together—whether we are walking, talking, traveling, dining with friends, or exchanging gossip and worries—all of it is valuable and puts me in touch with Borges' world, his thoughts, and his voice. Over the months, this has enabled me to determine not only how much of Borges' English I can use, but also what I must discard. Apart from its slightly old-fashioned and British qualities, which I affectionately term Edwardian and which are not really important, I am sometimes amazed to find him wavering about whether or not we should use a word like "direction," which he cannot believe is an everyday word. As for the gerund construction, whose use he abhors in his own language, I have had to convince him that it can be employed to advantage in English.

Time spent at Borges' side also helps me gauge his moods; now I can quickly detect (and sometimes deter him) when his inventive powers veer off into the non-serious or skyrocket into sheer clowning. Once, in the middle of a serious essay on the classics, I had to quit when Borges wanted to turn every other phrase into a Bustos Domecq joke.* Picking up again months later, with Borges in another mood, the work went smoothly. I have also learned to spot certain quirks—his aestheticism, for example, which will make him deliberately use a wrong word when the normal word sounds ugly to him. In a recent story, when he wrote of a house, "No puedo precisar su topografía"—literally, "I cannot fix its topography"—I knew at once that he really meant "location," but that in Buenos Aires usage "location" would be *ubicación*, a word he detests. Then there is his eccentric style of quoting words, sentences, and even paragraphs in italics rather than using quotation marks because he considers such marks uncouth; similarly, he will cite favorite works as though they were books of the Bible—that is, not troubling to set them in italics or to put quotation marks around them or to follow the other conventions for distinguishing a title. The following works have gained entrance into Borges' personal pantheon: Beowulf, the Ode to Brunanburh, the Divine Comedy, Macbeth, and Lugones' Lunario sentimental. (I have to admit that this particular idiosyncrasy—though I do not normally adopt it—is endearing.)

I must speak of my gratitude for Borges' irrepressible boyish humor, which pours a lot of sunshine into our work sessions and keeps us from taking ourselves too seriously. I have never known anyone quite so ready to make and take jokes about himself or his work. One example will do: we were once pondering a magazine editor's request for a more illuminating title than "Four Pieces" to cover the material his magazine had just accepted. Borges and I were dutifully serious for a long time, but no title came to us. Then we systematically began to consider and discuss what elements the pieces had in common. "I've got a title," I said finally: " 'No Mirrors or Mazes—a Tour de Force by Jorge Luis Borges.' "

"No, wait a moment," Borges said, "I think I have it: 'Mirrorless, Mazeless, Knifeless.' " After that the air was cleared, and at once a real title came.

III.

The work selected to illustrate our method of translation is "Pedro Salvadores," a

---

The Text: What, then, do we mean by a classic? I have within reach the definitions of Eliot, Matthew Arnold, Sainte-Beuve . . . .
Borges (suppressing a grin): How about "I have within reach the definitions of such worthies as . . ."?
di Giovanni: How about our strolling down Florida and getting ourselves some coffee instead?

tale set in Buenos Aires during the Rosas dictatorship over a hundred years ago. To escape certain death at the hands of the authorities, a man goes into hiding and lives nine years in the darkness of his own cellar. Borges wrote this story in June of 1969 for his book *Elogio de la sombra*. He had carried it in his head for some time, having first heard it from his mother, who had heard it from her father. In the fall of 1967, while at Harvard, Borges dictated three sentences of it in English to his secretary, John Murchison, and then laid it aside. The problem was to make the tale's complex background in Argentine history intelligible to the English-speaking reader. At the outset, Borges tells us that one of the three characters in the story is the dictator's "overpowering shadow," but because every Argentine knows who that dictator was, he is not mentioned by name except obliquely at the story's close. Similarly, a battle is mentioned without our being told its significance (again, Borges takes his reader's knowledge for granted, just as an American writer would not have to spell out the significance of Yorktown or Appomattox for his audience). We learn in passing that Salvadores is a Unitarian; we learn that a group of nightriders are the *mazorca*; and there is a mysterious reference to "blue chinaware." None of the terms or words is explained. How would we handle these vital details in the English version? Complicating matters still more was the fact that the story is so brief—it runs to no more than six or seven hundred words in the original—that any elucidation we intended to work into our English would have to be woven in very deftly. What was at stake here in the translation, I think, was the difference between reading two or three interesting pages, in which the general reader would never quite know what was going on, and reading a story that could be both understood and felt.

"A man, a woman, and the overpowering shadow of a dictator are the three characters," the second paragraph begins. The man was named Pedro Salvadores; Borges' grandfather had seen him days or weeks after the battle of Caseros. "What is the significance of the battle of Caseros?" I asked Borges at this point. "That was Rosas' downfall," Borges said. "Why don't we say that, then?" "Fine," agreed Borges, and with no more work than that, our first problem was solved. We wrote: "my grandfather Acevedo saw him days or weeks after the dictator's downfall in the battle of Caseros." The story continues: "Pedro Salvadores may have been no different from anyone else, but the years and his fate set him apart. He was a gentleman like many other gentlemen of his day. He owned (let us suppose) a ranch in the country and . . . ." Here we were in difficulty again. The Spanish at this point reads, "y era unitario"— "and was a Unitarian." Borges felt this would be lost on the American reader and should therefore be left out. But I was of another mind. I felt that if he supplied me with the background we could make the reference meaningful in English. I also felt it was absolutely essential to the piece that the sides be firmly established, and what better place than here. Salvadores was a Unitarian; Rosas a Federal. But we did not want to confuse matters by introducing a new term. I asked whether this meant Salvadores opposed the tyranny. The answer was yes. Then that's what we would say, and with the addition of four words we had a solution to the Unitarian problem. Pleased and amused, Borges ribbed me: "Now you're quite sure when they see Unitarian our readers won't be thinking Emerson and New England?" That I refused to guarantee, but now our translation ran: "He owned (let us suppose) a ranch in the country and, opposed to the tyranny, was on the Unitarian side."

It is at this juncture, in the sixth sentence of the paragraph, that Borges mentions the second character, the woman. We are told only that her family name was Planes; then the sentence goes on to say that Salvadores and his wife "vivían en la calle Suipacha, no lejos de la esquina del Temple"—"lived on Suipacha Street, not far from the corner of Temple." Without my asking, Borges immediately explained that Temple did not exist any more, that it was the old name for Viamonte. "But since these streets will mean nothing to the reader, you can leave them out if you want to," he said: "or instead, you might simply say 'in the heart of Buenos Aires.' " I argued with him that in reading English writers, though London streets meant little to me, I was grateful for their names all the same, since in my imagination they made London more real. He agreed that that was true, so we retained the names. But I liked his idea very much and thought we should use it as well; also, remembering things Borges had told me about the topography of old Buenos Aires—how the present Northside was once the edge of town—it occurred to me that if we worked in the one word "now" we could hint something about the spread of the city during the past century. We ended up with this: "they lived together on Suipacha Street near the corner of Temple in what is now the heart of Buenos Aires."

Next comes a description of their home, a typical Buenos Aires house of the day, "with a street door, long arched entranceway, inner grillwork gate" and "la hondura de los patios"—"a depth of patios." I was already familiar with this metaphor from one of Borges' poems, which we had worked on in Cambridge, and now of course, living in Buenos Aires, I knew firsthand what a depth of patios meant. Old Buenos Aires houses are narrow, extraordinarily deep affairs having a succession of patios. Borges often speaks of these. The first normally has black and white chessboard paving, and the third, which is usually unpaved, a grapevine. We decided the best way of expressing this was to speak of a "row of two or three patios."

In the Spanish text, the background information concludes here and the narrative begins. I felt, however, that something should be said about the dictator. Borges and I were in agreement that the American reader ought to be told who he was. At the head of the paragraph we learned that the characters were three; then we are given something about each of the first two. Here, then, to round out the presentation of the characters, was the place to mention Rosas. We simply added this short line to the story: "The dictator, of course, was Rosas." This, we felt, was also the natural place to conclude our paragraph and begin another.

"One night, around 1842," the new paragraph starts out, "Salvadores and his wife heard the growing, muffled sound of horses' hooves out on the unpaved street and the riders shouting their drunken *vivas* and their threats." Now comes the reference to the *mazorca*, which we would have to explain. The *mazorca*, it seemed to me after Borges described them, were the storm troopers of that era. The most straightforward solution we could think of was to say: "This time Rosas' henchmen did not ride on." Three sentences later, the word is used again, but having just been explained, we felt in this instance we could get away without translating or otherwise explaining it. The story continues:

> After the shouts came repeated knocks at the door; while the men began forcing it, Salvadores was able to pull the dining-room table aside, lift the rug, and hide himself down in the cellar. His wife dragged the table back in place. The *mazorca* broke into the house; they had come to take Salvadores. The woman said her husband had run away to Montevideo. The men did not believe her; they flogged her, they smashed all the blue chinaware. . . .

Here, with the mention of blue chinaware, was our last major problem, but it was only by chance that I found out it was a problem. Somehow, when I first read Borges' Spanish, "rompieron toda la vajilla celeste," my curiosity was aroused. Did he mean that they smashed *all* of Salvadores' chinaware, which happened to be blue, or was it that among all the crockery they smashed only the blue pieces? Only the blue, Borges told me, because blue was the Unitarian color. And when the Argentine reader sees "vajilla celeste," I wanted to know, does he understand at once what you are talking about? Yes, Borges said, everyone knew. In that case we would have to see that every American reader also knew. The best way to do this, I thought, was to insert the information between parentheses, particularly since Borges often uses the parenthesis in just this way. I wrote into the draft "(for blue was the color of the Unitarians)"; but as soon as the words were on the page, I saw how three of them could be cut. We ended up with this: "The men did not believe her; they flogged her, they smashed all the blue chinaware (blue was the Unitarian color), they searched the whole house, but they never thought of lifting the rug." From here on, the rest of "Pedro Salvadores" was fairly straight going. The whole of our work together on the translation was done in two short sessions; the story was published in English in the *New York Review of Books* before its first appearance in Spanish.

IV.

The worst difficulties in the translation of Borges' essays and other discursive work bear no relation to the problems of his fiction. In fact, the essays are such plain sailing that I am tempted to say that they present no real *translation* problems at all. But they very definitely present problems. What do you do, for instance, when you are nicely working your way through an essay on metaphor and you run across the following? "Let it suffice to recall that scene in Stevenson's last novel, *Weir of Hermiston*, in which the hero wants to find out whether Christina had a soul in her or 'si no es otra cosa que un animal del color de las flores.'" It is obviously out of the question to translate this back into English. Borges thought he remembered the exact words, but even in a man whose memory for literary quotations is phenomenal, the only way to do the job properly was to check against the original. I did. I found the nearest copy of *Weir of Hermiston* and began reading—and reading and reading. I have become fairly expert at digging out this sort of thing after the training afforded me by *The Book of Imaginary Beings*, but my performance here in the case of Stevenson was only middling. The ten words "if she were only an animal the colour of flowers" cost me about an hour's time.

Fortunately, Borges cites the majority of his sources, and sometimes when he hasn't he is able to give a fairly good idea what part of the text should be searched. But in this same essay on metaphor, a prayer of sailors on the Danube (and another of Phoenician sailors) had been quoted without any indication of the source. When I asked about it, Borges said he got it out of a Kipling story. He gave me a title for the story, but it was days before I could find it because in his memory he had confused the story's title and epigraph and given me the latter. Here the search for some thirteen or so words had turned into an adventure, for I had to ransack two libraries' holdings of Kipling before I stumbled across the explanation.

Quotations are not the only matter that have to be traced back to sources. Paraphrased material has also to be checked if the translated passage is to bear any resemblance to the subject matter under discussion. In "The Metaphor," an essay which is only about 1200 words long, the following books and authors had to be consulted: Snorri Sturluson, Benedetto Croce, Aristotle, Middleton Murry, the Bible, Kipling, Homer, Heine, Schopenhauer, Shakespeare, the *Mabinogion*, the *Nibelungenlied*, Ariosto, Tasso, Milton, Darío, Stevenson, Dante, and Góngora. It is no mystery, then, why I have come to believe that for a really first-rate translation of these essays, it is a good idea to be at Borges' side—especially to be helped out of pitfalls such as the Kipling one mentioned above. I wonder what two different American translators of Borges' story "The Intruder" made of that reference to the Bible fixed at the head of the tale. It is not an epigraph—no text is quoted. It simply says "2 Kings I, 26." A long time ago, in Cambridge, I had questioned Borges about this. There is no such passage in the Bible; that is to say, the first chapter of the Second Book of the Kings has only eighteen verses. I asked him if this were some game of his. No, he assured me, the passage existed all right, only the book he took it from also went under another name. At that moment, unfortunately, the other name escaped him. I later found it by reading the twenty-sixth verse of the first chapter of every book in the Bible until it turned up in the Second Book of Samuel, "otherwise called, The Second Book of the Kings." The next time I saw Borges I asked him why he had not affixed "2 Samuel I, 26" to the story. "Ah," he said, "but Kings is so much finer a word than Samuel, don't you think?"

Early in 1969, Borges and I translated his *Book of Imaginary Beings*. It is a volume containing over a hundred miniature essays—or rather, essays and pseudo-essays, for a number of the pieces are of Borges' own invention. These pieces run anywhere from five lines to four pages long. It was this book that sharpened my technique of perusing a classic so as, in ten minutes' time, to come up with the sought-after quotation. In fact, in addition to providing me with a whole education in out-of-the-way learning, the book made me familiar with every library in Buenos Aires and put me on especially intimate terms with the basement of Argentina's Biblioteca Nacional. Even today, after all these intervening months, I can lay my hand on almost any volume of the Loeb Classical Library in semidarkness.

Our work on *The Book of Imaginary Beings* started out as a straight translation; we soon found, however, that we would have to make a new edition of it. First, so many of Borges' original sources were in English that we found it desirable and easy to lengthen some of the quotations he had initially had to work hard at translating into Spanish. This forced us to do some rewriting. Next, we found that the Argentine printers had made so many mistakes in the text we were translating that there was very little we could take on faith. Names of persons and towns were spelled incorrectly, dates were wrong, quotations were misquoted, and citations were wrongly cited. This meant that a large part of the research had to be redone. Once we had gone this far, we found it necessary to alter many of the articles, correcting and revising material or adding interesting bits of information that we kept turning up in our new investigations. When we finished with the book's 116 pieces, Borges insisted that we have some fun as a reward for our labors, so we included some new ones. We compiled two on South American fauna and then tried our hands at inventing two more. Borges was so pleased with the total result of the new book that he insists that any future translations of his bestiary into other languages be done from our English-language edition. After the translation was mailed to our American publisher, I presented the Buenos Aires publisher with a corrected copy of the Spanish text. Its approximately 150 pages had extended hospitality to 103 errors.

There is something about Borges' modesty and quiet manner and his complete inability to make the smallest requests, let alone any sort of demand, that have the personal effect of spurring me to greater efforts—especially in taking pains to get things right. We were translating the part in *The Book of Imaginary Beings* that we came to call "An Offspring of Leviathan." In the Spanish text, this consisted of an excerpt of about a hundred words, cited from a French source. Borges told me that although he had made his translation into Spanish from the French, the piece had first been written in Latin. This information immediately discouraged me about the draft I had already made of the piece from the Spanish, so I combed the National Library for the original Latin text. The book containing it was a thirteenth-century compendium of the lives of saints, called the *Golden Legend*. It was in medieval Latin, around nine hundred pages long, and its type was the size of newsprint. Still worse, the book had no index, nor did I have any notion of which saint I was looking for. I took the volume home and began scanning the pages, line by line, with my eye ready to pick out a couple of capitalized words—Rhone and Avignon—that occurred at the beginning of the excerpt. After nearly two hours I managed to spot the passage on page 444. The next day Borges and I prepared a new version straight from the Latin. Of course, there were some differences between my first version from the Spanish and this new one from the Latin. The second was definitely sharper, although it was really not extremely different. We could easily have got by with the first, but if we had I am sure we would have lost the pleasure the work gave us—in this case, locating the text, making our fresh version, and in the end deciding to introduce the quotation with a dozen lines about the *Golden Legend*. It is pleasing to please Borges; and it perhaps follows that if we are able to create these pleasures for ourselves, we may stir up similar enthusiasm in our readers.

Sometimes these extra efforts lead us to strange and wonderful occurrences. Late one afternoon, during a thunderstorm, we were at the library searching for a poem by Victor Hugo which Borges wanted to write about in our revised article on "The Jinn." There was a power failure and suddenly we were without lights. After a time, everyone —readers and staff—left the building. But the watchman lent me a weak flashlight so that Borges and I could prowl the stacks looking for Hugo's poems. I had checked call numbers in the catalog, but they were useless without the staff, because the National Library has a peculiar system of shelving books according to size, not subject. This meant that Hugo might have been anywhere among the 800,000 volumes. Nonetheless, Borges and I started out in the dark in search of our book. Something made us walk through the first floor stacks and start for the next level. The stairway split, branching right and left. Something impelled me to the left. When we got to the head of the stairway, I was forced to pause a moment for Borges, who was on my arm half a step behind me. As I did so, the beam of my light came to rest on a set of Hugo's complete works, and in the first volume we took down we found the reference. Who could tell what power had led us so unhesitatingly to the poem we blindly sought. "Isn't this a stroke of luck?" I said.

"I think we'd best be leaving with our book now," Borges said; "the word for this is uncanny."

Buenos Aires

[Appendix]

*Pedro Salvadores**

I want to leave a written record (perhaps the first to be attemped) of one of the strangest and grimmest happenings in Argentine history. To meddle as little as possible in the telling, to abstain from picturesque details or personal conjectures is, it seems to me, the only way to do this.

A man, a woman, and the overpowering shadow of a dictator are the three characters. The man's name was Pedro Salvadores; my grandfather Acevedo saw him

---

*Reprinted with permission from *The Aleph and Other Stories*, New York, Dutton, 1970, pp. 187–89. Translated by Norman Thomas di Giovanni in collaboration with the author.

days or weeks after the dictator's downfall in the battle of Caseros. Pedro Salvadores may have been no different from anyone else, but the years and his fate set him apart. He was a gentleman like many other gentlemen of his day. He owned (let us suppose) a ranch in the country and, opposed to the tyranny, was on the Unitarian side. His wife's family name was Planes; they lived together on Suipacha Street near the corner of Temple in what is now the heart of Buenos Aires. The house in which the event took place was much like any other, with its street door, long arched entranceway, inner grillwork gate, its rooms, its row of two or three patios. The dictator, of course, was Rosas.

One night, around 1842, Salvadores and his wife heard the growing, muffled sound of horses' hooves out on the unpaved street and the riders shouting their drunken *vivas* and their threats. This time Rosas' henchmen did not ride on. After the shouts came repeated knocks at the door; while the men began forcing it, Salvadores was able to pull the dining-room table aside, lift the rug, and hide himself down in the cellar. His wife dragged the table back in place. The *mazorca* broke into the house; they had come to take Salvadores. The woman said her husband had run away to Montevideo. The men did not believe her; they flogged her, they smashed all the blue chinaware (blue was the Unitarian color), they searched the whole house, but they never thought of lifting the rug. At midnight they rode away, swearing that they would soon be back.

Here is the true beginning of Pedro Salvadores' story. He lived nine years in the cellar. For all we may tell ourselves that years are made of days and days of hours and that nine years is an abstract term and an impossible sum, the story is nonetheless grue-some. I suppose that in the darkness, which his eyes somehow learned to decipher, he had no particular thoughts, not even of his hatred or his danger. He was simply there —in the cellar—with echoes of the world he was cut off from sometimes reaching him from overhead: his wife's footsteps, the bucket clanging against the lip of the well, a heavy rainfall in the patio. Every day of his imprisonment, for all he knew, could have been the last.

His wife let go all the servants, who could possibly have informed against them, and told her family that Salvadores was in Uruguay. Meanwhile, she earned a living for them both sewing uniforms for the army. In the course of time, she gave birth to two children; her family turned from her, thinking she had a lover. After the tyrant's fall, they got down on their knees and begged to be forgiven.

What was Pedro Salvadores? Who was he? Was it his fear, his love, the unseen presence of Buenos Aires, or—in the long run—habit that held him prisoner? In order to keep him with her, his wife would make up news to tell him about whispered plots and rumored victories. Maybe he was a coward and she loyally hid it from him that she knew. I picture him in his cellar perhaps without a candle, without a book. Dark-ness probably sank him into sleep. His dreams, at the outset, were probably of that sudden night when the blade sought his throat, of the streets he knew so well, of the open plains. As the years went on, he would have been unable to escape even in his sleep; whatever he dreamed would have taken place in the cellar. At first, he may have been a man hunted down, a man in danger of his life; later (we will never know for certain), an animal at peace in its burrow or a sort of dim god.

All this went on until that summer day of 1852 when Rosas fled the country. It was only then that the secret man came out into the light of day; my grandfather spoke with him. Flabby, overweight, Salvadores was the color of wax and could not speak above a low voice. He never got back his confiscated lands; I think he died in poverty.

As with so many things, the fate of Pedro Salvadores strikes us as a symbol of something we are about to understand, but never quite do.

Borges in Oklahoma 1969

By IVAR IVASK

Borges Oklahomas 1969[*]

Poolpime kentaur
kes oma keerdkäike
kannab endaga ikka
aastatuhandetepikkuse
mäluga Homeros
ja siiski siiski
veri me ehmund verest
vaim me nördind vaimust
igavesse eksiili saadetud

Borges in Oklahoma 1969

Centaur
half-blinded
coursing
your meandering route
Homer
of millennial memory
and yet
blood of our startled blood
spirit of our furious spirit
forever banished

Borges en Oklahoma 1969

Un centauro cegato
que se acompaña
de sus propios laberintos
Homero
con memoria de milenios
y sin embargo
sangre de nuestra aterrada sangre
espíritu de nuestro airado espíritu
enviado al destierro eterno

Spanish Translation by Manuel Mantero

---

[*]This Estonian poem has been rendered in English by the author, with some helpful suggestions from Tom J. Lewis.

Jorge Luis Borges at the University of Oklahoma, December, 1969.

Toward a Bibliography on Jorge Luis Borges (1923-1969)

By ROBERT L. FIORE

Among contemporary Hispanic writers Jorge Luis Borges is perhaps the most widely known. Because of the great interest in Borges, this bibliography has been prepared with the hope that it may facilitate scholarly investigation of his literary works.

Since new studies on Borges appear constantly, no bibliography can include all that has been written. The list that follows does not aspire to be complete, hence the title *Toward a Bibliography on Jorge Luis Borges (1923–1969)*. The bibliographies of Ana María Barrenechea, Nodier Lucio and Lydia Revello, and the one included in the *Cahier* dedicated to Borges published by *L'Herne* have proved to be useful. The present study is an attempt to verify, to correct, and to add to the bibliographical data previously published. Included in an *addendum* are entries which have not been verified because of lack of information.

I wish to thank my colleague Donald A. Yates, who has supplied me with several articles which would have been impossible to obtain without his help. I wish also to express my appreciation to Michigan State University for the All-University grant which supported the research on which this bibliography is based.

A

———"El cicerone del laberinto," *Primera Plana* (Buenos Aires), 18 al 24 de marzo de 1969, pág. 68.

———"Jorge Luis Borges, mágico jinete," *Correo Literario*, Núm. 3 (1954).

A. G. "Ficciones," *Contrapunto* (Buenos Aires), I, Núm. 2 (1945).

Abadi, Marcelo N. "Borges o de la filosofía argentina," *Revista Centro* (Buenos Aires, Núm. 14 (octubre-diciembre de 1959), págs. 170-176.

Aguirre, J. M. "La solución a la adivinanza propuesta por Jorge Luis Borges," *Bulletin of Hispanic Studies*, XLII (1965), 174-181.

Alazraki, Jaime. "Borges y el problema del estilo," *Revista Hispánica Moderna*, XXXIII (1967), 204-215.

———"Las figuras de contigüidad en la prosa narrativa de Borges," *Revista Ibérica*, XXXIV (1968), 45-66.

———*La prosa narrativa de Jorge Luis Borges*. Madrid, Gredos, 1968.

Albano, Mario. "Atisbo de interpretación argentina: Jorge Luis Borges," *Sur*, Núm. 169 (noviembre de 1948), págs. 61-64.

Albérès, René Marill. "J. L. Borges ou les deux bouts du monde," *Affinités* (Buenos Aires), II, Núm. 7 (abril de 1953), 84-85 y 92.

Alcalay, Jaime. *De Swift a Borges*. Buenos Aires, Galatea, 1967.

Alcorta, Gloria. "Desagravio a Borges," *Sur*, Núm. 94 (julio de 1942), pág. 20.

Alonso, Amado. "Borges, narrador," *Sur*, Núm. 14 (noviembre de 1935), págs. 105-115.

————"Borges, narrador," en su *Materia y forma en poesía* (Madrid, Gredos, 1955), págs. 434-449.

————"Desagravio a Borges," *Sur*, Núm. 94 (julio de 1942), págs. 15-17.

————"Desagravio a Borges," en su *Materia y forma en poesía* (Madrid, Gredos, 1955), págs. 450-452.

————"Discusión sobre Jorge Luis Borges," *Megáfono*, Núm. 11 (agosto de 1933), pág. 19.

————"Polémica: a quienes leyeron a Jorge Luis Borges en *Sur*, Núm. 86," *Sur*, Núm. 89 (febrero de 1942), págs. 79-81.

Amorim, Enrique. "Desagravio a Borges," *Sur*, Núm. 94 (julio de 1942), págs. 29-30.

Anderson Imbert, Enrique. "Un cuento de Borges: 'La casa de Asterión'," *Revista Iberoamericana*, XXV, Núm. 40 (1960), 33-43.

————"Un cuento de Borges: 'La casa de Asterión'," en su *Crítica Interna* (Madrid, Taurus, 1960), págs. 247-249. También en *Revista Iberoamericana*, XXV (1960), 33-43.

————"Desagravio a Borges," *Sur*, Núm. 94 (julio de 1942), págs. 24-25.

————"Discusión sobre Jorge Luis Borges," *Megáfono*, Núm. 11 (agosto de 1933), págs. 28-29.

————"Jorge Luis Borges," *Revista de la Universidad de México*, VIII, Núm. 4 (diciembre de 1953).

————"Jorge Luis Borges," en *Historia de la literatura hispanoamericana* (México, Fondo de Cultura Económica, 1954), pág. 89; 2ª ed., 1957, págs. 382-384; 3ª ed., 1961, II, 228-233.

————"Nueva contribución al estudio de las fuentes de Borges," *Filología*, VIII (1962; publicado en 1964), 7-13.

Andries, Marc. "De Liefdes van Borges," *De Nieuwe Stem*, XXI (1966), 565-567.

Anzoátegui, Ignacio B. "Discusión sobre Jorge Luis Borges," *Megáfono*, Núm. 11 (agosto de 1933), págs. 16-17.

Ardiles Gray, Julio. "Conversación acerca de Borges," *La Gaceta* (Tucumán), 10 de abril de 1954.

Arfini, Alfredo. *Borges: pobre ciego balbuciente*. Rosario, Librería y editorial Ruiz, 1968.

Arreola, Juan José. "Jorge Luis Borges y las literaturas germánicas," *Revista de la Universidad de México*, VI, Núm. 65 (mayo de 1952).

Ayala, Juan Antonio. "Un planeamiento estructural en Jorge Luis Borges," *Vida Universitaria* (Monterrey), 12 de abril de 1964.

Azancot, Leopoldo. "Borges y Kafka," *Indice*, XVII, Núm. 170 (1963), 6.

————"Justificación de Borges," *Indice*, XVII, Núm. 170 (1963), 6.

B. de V. "Los guapos de Borges en el cine nacional," *La Nación* (Buenos Aires), 21 de septiembre de 1961.

Bagby, Albert I., II. "The Concept of Time in Jorge Luis Borges," *Romance Notes*, VI (1965), 99-105.

B

Barahona Aguayo, Rosaura. "Las ruinas circulares," *Armas y Letras*, V, Núms. 1-2 (1962), 46-55.

Barfod, Einar. "Postulación de Jorge Luis Borges," *Marcha* (Montevideo), 21 de junio de 1957.

Barletta, Leónidas. "Desagravio a Borges," *Argentina Libre* (Buenos Aires), 25 de julio de 1946.

——"Las dos caras de Borges," *Propósitos* (Montevideo), 18 de abril de 1968, págs. 1-2.

Barrenechea, Ana María. "Borges y el lenguaje," *Nueva Revista de Filología Hispánica*, VII, Núms. 3-4 (1953), 551-569.

——*Borges, the Labyrinth Maker*. Tr. y Ed. Robert Lima. New York, N. Y. University Press, 1965.

——*La expresión de la irrealidad en la obra de Jorge Luis Borges*. México, El Colegio de México, 1957. Otra Edición, Buenos Aires, Paidós, 1967.

——"La expresión de la irrealidad en la obra de Jorge Luis Borges," en Barrenechea, A. M. y Speratti Piñero, Emma Susana, *La literatura fantástica en Argentina* (México, Impr. Universitaria, 1957), 54-72.

——"Una ficción de Jorge Luis Borges," *Revista de la Universidad de México*, VIII, Núm. 12 (agosto de 1954), 15, 20.

——"El infinito en la obra de Jorge Luis Borges," *Nueva Revista de Filología Hispánica*, X, Núm. 1 (1956), 13-35.

——"El tiempo y la eternidad en la obra de Borges," *Revista Hispánica Moderna*, XXIII, Núm. 1 (1957), 28-41.

Barth, John. "The Literature of Exhaustion," *Atlantic*, CCXX, No. 2 (August, 1967), págs. 29-34.

Bartholomew, Roy. *Cien poesías rioplatenses, 1800-1950; antología*. Buenos Aires, Raigal, 1954. Sobre Borges, págs. 286-287.

——"Nota [a propósito de Borges y la nueva generación, de Adolfo Prieto]," *Ciudad*, Núms. 2-3 (1955), págs. 93-101.

Batis, Huberto. " 'El muerto': cuento de Jorge Luis Borges," *Universidad de México*, XII, Núm. 2 (octubre de 1957), 13-16.

Becco, Horacio Jorge. Véase Ríos Patrón, José Luis.

Beck, Vera F. "La revista Martín Fierro: rememoración de su XXV aniversario," *Revista Hispánica Moderna*, XVI (1950), 133-141.

Bénichou, Paul. "Kublai Khan, Coleridge y Borges," *Sur*, Núm. 236 (septiembre-octubre de 1955), págs. 57-61.

——"Le monde de José [sic] Luis Borges," *Critique* (Paris), VIII, Núms. 63-64 (agosto-septiembre de 1952), 675-687.

——"Le monde et l'esprit chez Jorge Luis Borges," *Les Lettres Nouvelles* (Paris), II, Núm. 21 (noviembre de 1954), 680-699.

Benoist, Jean Marie. "Le jeu de J. L. Borges." *Critique*, XXIV, (1968), 654-73.

Bernárdez, Francisco Luis. "Un Borges de entrecasa," *Martín Fierro*, 2 ep., III, Núm. 33 (septiembre de 1926), 8.

——"Dos poetas, dos conductas estéticas," *Criterio* (Buenos Aires), XXVII, Núm. 1220 (23 de septiembre de 1956), 716.

——"Jorge Luis Borges," *La Nación* (Buenos Aires), 13 de diciembre de 1925.

Bianco, José. "Desagravio a Borges," *Sur*, Núm. 94 (julio de 1942), págs. 23-24.

Bienek, Horst. "Biographie eines Dichters," *Merkur*, XVIII (1964), 242-246.

Bietti, Oscar. "Jorge Luis Borges, el hacedor," *La Prensa* (Buenos Aires), 30 de julio de 1961.

Bioy Casares, Adolfo. "Desagravio a Borges," *Sur*, Núm. 94 (julio de 1942), pág. 22.

———" 'El jardín de los senderos que se bifurcan'," *CEA; Centro de Editoriales Argentinas*, I, Núm. 4 (1943), 17-18.

———"Jorge Luis Borges: 'El jardín de los senderos que se bifurcan'," *Sur*, Núm. 92 (mayo de 1942), págs. 60-65.

Blanco Amores de Pagella, Angela. "Los temas esenciales en la poesía de Borges," *Cursos y Conferencias*, LVI, Núm. 288 (1960), 137-147.

Blanco-González, Manuel. *Jorge Luis Borges, anotaciones sobre el tiempo en su obra*. Mexico, Andrea, 1963.

Blanco-Fombona, Manuel. "Jorge Luis Borges," *South American Journal* (London), CXLVI, Núm. 1 (July 2, 1949), 6.

Bock, Werner. "Begegnungen mit Jorge Luis Borges," *Humbolt; revista para el mundo ibérico* (Hamburg), II, Núm. 6 (1961), 98-99.

Borello, Rodolfo A. "Estructura de la prosa de Jorge L. Borges," *Cuadernos Hispanoamericanos*, LV (1963), 485-494.

Bosco, María Angélica. *Borges y los otros*. Buenos Aires, Fabril, 1967.

Botsford, Keith. "About Borges and Not about Borges," *Kenyon Review*, XXVI (1964), 723-737.

———"Sobre y al margen de Jorge Luis Borges," *Revista Mexicana Literatura*, 5/6 (1964), 43-61.

Brion, Marcel. "D'un autre hémisphère," *Le Monde* (Paris), 26 de marzo de 1952.

———"J. L. Borges et ses Labyrinthes," *Le Monde* (Paris), 18 de agosto de 1954.

Brughetti, Romualdo. "Una nueva generación literaria argentina, 1940-50," *Cuadernos Americanos*, LXVIII (1952).

Brumana, Herminia C. "Borges, conferencista," *Sur*, Núms. 209-210 (marzo-abril de 1952), págs. 185-187.

Bullrich, Silvina. "El misterio de la literatura," *Atlántida* (Buenos Aires), abril de 1952, pág. 45.

Burgin, Richard. *Conversations with Jorge Luis Borges*. New York, Holt, Rinehart and Winston, 1968.

———"A Conversation with Borges," *Partisan Review*, XXXVI, No. 1 (Winter, 1969), 112-122.

Caillois, Roger. "Rectificación a una nota de Jorge Luis Borges," *Sur*, Núm. 91 (abril de 1942), págs. 71-72.

———*Sociología de la novela*. Buenos Aires, *Sur*, 1944.

———"Soldats de la Liberté!" *Opera* (Paris), 30 de enero de 1952.

Calzadilla, Juan. "Poemas, por Jorge Luis Borges," *Revista Nacional de Cultura* (Caracas), Núm. 131 (1958), págs. 160-161.

Campos, Jorge. "Las ficciones de Borges," *Insula*, XVI, Núm. 175 (1962), 11.

———Sobre: *Historia de la eternidad, Insula* (Madrid), Núm. 110 (febrero de 1955).

Canal Feijóo, Bernardo. "Dédalo y los titanes escépticos," *Reseña* (Buenos Aires), Núm. 3 (agosto de 1949).

C

————"Desagravio a Borges," *Sur*, Núm. 94 (julio de 1942), págs. 32-34.

Cañas, Salvador. "Alma fuerte en el concepto de Jorge Luis Borges," *Síntesis*, II, Núm. 14 (1955), 23-26.

Cansinos-Asséns, Rafael. *La nueva literatura*. Tomo III: *La evolución de la poesía (1917-1927)*. Madrid, Páez, 1927. Sobre Borges: págs. 280-302.

————"Sobre Borges en España: Impresión de una visita," *Indice de Artes y Letras*, XVII, Núm. 170 (1963), 5.

Canto, Estela. "Güiraldes fué la cantárida de Florida, afirma Mastronardi," *Nueva Gaceta* (Buenos Aires), 7 de noviembre de 1949.

————"Jorge Luis Borges, *El Aleph*," *Sur*, Núm. 180 (octubre de 1949), págs. 93-98.

Canto, Patricio. "Desagravio a Borges," *Sur*, Núm. 94 (julio de 1942), pág. 13.

Capasso, Maddalena. "Un motivo sentimentale nella poesia di Jorge Luis Borges," en *Studi di letteratura, storia e filosofia in onore di Bruno Revel* (Firenze, 1965), págs. 129-133.

Capdevila, Arturo. "Discurso de don Arturo Capdevila en la recepción académica de don Jorge Luis Borges," *Boletín de la Academia Argentina de Letras*, XXVII (1962), 297-301.

Capsus, Cleon Wade. "The Poetry of Jorge Luis Borges," *Dissertation Abstracts*, XXV (1965), 4697.

Carella, Tulio. "Jorge Luis Borges y A. Bioy Casares: Libro de cielo y del infierno," *Sur*, Núm. 271 (1961), págs. 83-85.

Carilla, Emilio. "Un cuento de Borges," *Estudios de literatura argentina* (Tucumán, Facultad de Filosofía y Letras de la Universidad Nacional, 1961), págs. 21-32.

————"Un cuento de Borges," *Studia philologica; homenaje ofrecido a Dámaso Alonso por sus amigos y discípulos con ocasión de su 60° aniversario* (Madrid, Gredos, 1960), I, 295-306.

————"Un poema de Borges," *Revista Hispánica Moderna*, XXIX (1963), 32-45.

————"El vanguardismo en la Argentina," *Estudios de literatura argentina* (Tucumán, Facultad de Filosofía y Letras de la Universidad Nacional, 1961), págs. 61-103.

Carlos, Alberto J. "Dante y *El Aleph* de Borges," *Duquesne Hispanic Review*, V (1966), 35-50.

Carpeaux, Otto María. "O mundo fantástico de J. L. Borges," *Presenças* (Río de Janeiro, Instituto nacional do livro, 1958), págs. 134-138.

Carreño, Virginia. "Comienzos literarios de Borges en francés," *Affinités* (Buenos Aires), XII, Núm. 44 (diciembre de 1962), 26-27, 67.

Carrouges, Michel. "Le gai savoir de Jorge Luis Borges," *Preuves* (Paris), Núm. 13 (1952), págs. 47-49.

Casulla, Luis. Sobre *El Aleph*, *Espiga* (Rosario), III, Núms. 8-9 (1950).

Cecchi, Emilio. "Impresiones italianas sobre Jorge Luis Borges," *La Nación* (Buenos Aires), 24 de mayo de 1964.

Charbonnier, Georges. *Entretiens avec Jorge Luis Borges*. Paris, Gallimard, 1967.

Chourmouziadis, G. D. "Jorge Luis Borges: Henas magos tou logou." *Nea Hestia*, LXXXII (1967), 1609-1613.

Christ, Ronald. "Borges Translated," *The Nation* (March 1, 1971), 282-284.

————"Interview with Borges," *Paris Review* (Winter-Spring, 1967).

————*The Narrow Act: Borges' Art of Allusion*. New York, New York University Press, 1969.

Chumacero, Alí. "La poesía de Borges," *Letras Mexicanas* (México), IV, Núm. 19 (1944).

Chumillas, Ventura. "Jorge Luis Borges," *El Pueblo* (Buenos Aires), 9 de febrero de 1930.

Clemente, José Edmundo. "Borges íntimo," *La Nación* (Buenos Aires), 7 de mayo de 1961.

——*Estética del lector*. Buenos Aires, El Ateneo, 1950.

Cócaro, Nicolás. ——, *Oeste* (Buenos Aires), X, Núm. 17 (1954).

Codignola, Luciano. Sobre: "La biblioteca di Babele," *Tempo Presente* (Roma), I, Núm. 2 (mayo de 1956), 178.

Cohen, J. M. "Two Argentine Poets, Ricardo Molinari and J. L. Borges," *Atlante* (London), I (1953), 87-88.

Concha, Edmundo. "Jorge Luis Borges o la literatura para minorías," *Atenea*, CXXXII, Núm. 382 (1958), 183-186.

Córdova Iturburu, Cayetano. "El movimiento de la generación de la revista *Martín Fierro*," *Espiga* (Rosario), III, Núms. 8-9 (1950).

Correia Pacheco, Armando. "Jorge Luis Borges, escritor universal de América," *Revista de la Universidad* (La Plata), Núm. 16 (1962), págs. 184-188.

Cortínez, Carlos. "Con Borges," *Anales de la Universidad de Chile*, CXXV, Núms. 141-144 (enero-diciembre de 1967), 135-145.

Corvalán, Octavio. "Borges, narrador y erudito," en *Modernismo y Vanguardia* (New York, Las Américas, 1967), págs. 208-216.

——"Presencia de Buenos Aires en 'La muerte y la brújula' de Jorge Luis Borges," *Revista Iberoamericana*, XXVIII (1962), 359-363.

Costa Alvarez, Arturo. "*El idioma de los argentinos* por Jorge Luis Borges," *Nosotros* (Buenos Aires), XXII, Núm. 230, tomo 61 (1928), 125-127.

Cro, Stelio. "Borges e Dante," *Lettere Italiane*, XX (1968), 403-410.

——"Jorge Luis Borges e Miguel de Unamuno," *Annali di Ca' Foscari* (Venezia), VI (1967), 81-90.

D Dauster, Frank. "La antología personal de Borges," *Revista Hispánica Moderna*, XXIX (1963), 162-163.

——"Notes on Borges' Labyrinths," *Hispanic Review*, XXX (1962), 142-148.

Debicki, Andrew P. "Nota sobre la ironía en algunos poemas de Borges," *Duquesne Hispanic Review*, III (1964), 49-56.

De Lellis, Jorge Mario. "Necesidad de una poética nacional," *La Prensa* (Buenos Aires), 21 de septiembre de 1954.

de Man, Paul. "A Modern Master," *New York Review of Books*, Nov. 19, 1964, págs. 8-10.

Devoto, Daniel. "Del gran inquisidor," *Buenos Aires Literaria*, I, Núm. 1 (octubre de 1952), págs. 47-50.

Diego, Celia de. "La sinrazón razonada de los parricidas," *Ficción* (Buenos Aires), Núm. 12 (marzo-abril de 1958), págs. 90-99.

Diehl, Adán C. "Desagravio a Borges," *Sur*, Núm. 94 (julio de 1942), págs. 25-26.

Díez-Canedo, Enrique. Sobre *El Fervor de Buenos Aires*, *España* (Madrid), X, Núm. 168 (15 de marzo de 1924).

——Sobre *El Fervor de Buenos Aires*, *Letras de América; estudios sobre las literaturas continentales* (México, El Colegio de México, 1944), págs. 369-372.

———Sobre *El Fervor de Buenos Aires, Nosotros* (Buenos Aires), XVII, Núm. 46 (1924), 433-434.

di Giovanni, Norman Thomas. "On Translating Borges," *Encounter* (London), XXXII (April 1969), 22-24.

Dizzionario universale della letteratura contemporanea. Milano, Mondadori, 1959. Sobre Borges: I, 503-504.

Doll, Ramón. "Discusiones con Borges, una encuesta," *Letras*, 2ª éd. (Buenos Aires), III, Núm. 1 (septiembre de 1933), 3-13.

Dondo, Osvaldo Horacio. "Jorge Luis Borges," *Péñola* (Buenos Aires), I, Núm. 3 (junio de 1939), 42-49.

Doreste, Ventura. "Borges y la zoología fantástica," *Insula*, XIII, Núm. 142 (1958), 5.

Drieu-La-Rochelle, Pierre. "Discusión sobre Jorge Luis Borges," *Megáfono*, Núm. 11 (agosto de 1933), págs. 13-14.

———"Jorge Luis Borges; le poète et la ville," *Sur les Ecrivains* (Paris, Gallimard, 1964).

Dulsey, Bernard. "An Interview with Jorge Luis Borges," *American Book Collector*, XIII, Núm. 6 (1963), 19-20.

Durán, Manuel. "Jorge Luis Borges," *Forjadores del mundo moderno* (México), VII (1961), 309-317.

———"Los dos Borges," *La Palabra y el Hombre*, Núm. 27 (1963), págs. 417-423.

Durand, José. "De Lugones a Borges," *Novedades*, 17 de febrero de 1952.

E. J. M. "Un gran libro en su tercera década de vida," *La Nación* (Buenos Aires), 28 de diciembre de 1958.

E. M. "La nueva revista *Proa*," *Martín Fierro*, 2ª ép., I, Núms. 8-9 (agosto-septiembre de 1924), 9.

Eichelbaum, Samuel. "Desagravio a Borges," *Sur*, Núm. 94 (julio de 1942), págs. 20-21.

Enguídanos, Miguel. "Correspondencia," *Revista de la Universidad de México*, XVI, Núm. 11 (julio de 1962), 11.

———"El criollismo de Borges," *Papeles de Son Armadans* (Palma de Mallorca), XXXIII (1964), 17-32.

———"Imaginación y evasión en los cuentos de Jorge Luis Borges," *Papeles de Son Armadans* (Palma de Mallorca), X (1958), 233-251.

———"Imagination and Escape in the Short Stories of Jorge Luis Borges," *Texas Quarterly*, IV (1961), 118-127.

———"Introducción a *El hacedor*," *Sur*, Núm. 285 (1963), págs. 89-91.

Estrella Gutiérrez, Fermín. "Borges." *Revista Nacional de Cultura* (Caracas), CLXXXI (1967), 54-59.

———*Panorama sintético de la literatura argentina.* Santiago de Chile, Ercilla, 1938. Sobre Borges: págs. 33-44 y 96-97.

Etcheverry, J. E. Sobre Ana María Barrenechea, *La expresión de la irrealidad en la obra de Jorge Luis Borges, Revista Iberoamericana de Literatura,* I (1959), 111-112.

Etiemble. "Un homme à tuer: Jorge Luis Borges, cosmopolite," *Les Temps Modernes* (Paris), VIII, Núm. 83 (1952), 512-526.

———"Un homme à tuer: Jorge Luis Borges, cosmopolite," en su *Hygiène des lettres*, II (Paris, 1955), págs. 120-141.

E

F

F. L. B. "Un Borges de entrecasa," *Martín Fierro,* Núm. 33 (3 de septiembre de 1926).

Fernández Moreno, César. "Esquemas de Borges," *Ciudad,* Núms. 2-3 (1955), págs. 11-13.

———*Esquemas de Borges.* Buenos Aires, Perrot, 1957.

———"La poesía argentina de vanguardia," en Arrieta, Rafael Alberto, dir. *Historia de la literatura argentina* (Buenos Aires, Peuser, 1958-60), IV, 605-665.

———"Poesía argentina desde 1920," *Cuadernos Americanos,* V. Núm. 5 (1946), 230 y ss.

———*La realidad y los papeles.* Buenos Aires, Aguilar, 1967.

———"Los relatos de Jorge Luis Borges," *Sur,* Núm. 125 (marzo de 1945), págs. 69-78.

———"Weary of Labyrinths," *Encounter* (London), XXXIII (April, 1969), 3-14.

Ferreira, João-Francisco. "Poesía de vanguarda," en su *Capítulos de literatura hispanoamericana* (Pörto Alegre, Faculdade de Filosofía, 1959), págs. 386-411.

Ferrer, Manuel. "Borges y la nada." *Dissertation Abstracts,* XXVIII (1968), 5051A (Wisconsin).

Flores, Angel. "Magical Realism in Spanish American Fiction," *Hispania,* XXXVIII (1955), 187-192.

Florit, Eugenio. "Jorge Luis Borges: *Ficciones,*" *Revista Hispánica Moderna,* XIII, Núms. 1-2 (1947), 64-65.

Forcada Cabanellas, M. "Poetas ultraístas," en *De la vida literaria; testimonios de una época* (Rosario, Ciencia, 1941), págs. 61-83.

Foster, David William. "Borges and Dis-Reality: An Introduction to His Poetry," *Hispania,* XLV (1962), 625-629.

———"Borges' *El Aleph*: Some Thematic Considerations," *Hispania,* XLVIII (1964), 56-59.

Freden, Gustaf. "Jorge Luis Borges, Rationalist och mystiker," *Göteborgs Handels och Sjöfartstidning* (Göteborg), 11 de junio, 1954.

Fuentes, Pedro Miguel. "Borges y Borges," *Estudios,* Núm. 532 (1962), págs. 127-131.

G

G. R. C. Sobre *El Aleph, Vida Hispánica* (London), IV, Núm. 1 (mayo de 1950).

Gallardo Drago, Miguel. "Lo mejor de Borges, según J. L. Borges," *La Nación* (Buenos Aires), 24 de junio de 1962.

Gallo, Ugo. *Storia della letteratura Ispano Americana.* Milano, Nuova accademia editrice, 1954. Sobre Borges: págs. 428-430.

García, Germán. *La novela argentina; un itinerario.* Buenos Aires, Sud Americana, 1952. Sobre Borges: págs. 220-221 y 283.

García Cantú, G. "De Granados a Borges," *Novedades* (México), 9 de junio de 1957.

García Pinto, Roberto. "Un poema de Borges," *Autores y personajes* (Tucumán, Facultad de Filosofía y Letras de la Universidad Nacional, 1961), págs. 57-60.

———"Un poema de Borges," *Sur,* Núm. 253 (julio-agosto de 1958), págs. 69-71.

García Ponce, Juan. "¿Quien es Borges?" *Revista Mexicana Literatura*, Núms. 5/6 (1964), págs. 23-42.

García Torres, Jaime. "La feria de los días [una nueva carta de Enguídanos a próposito de J. L. Borges]," *Revista de la Universidad de México*, XVI (1962), Núm. 10, pág. 13; Núm. 12, pág. 3.

Gass, William H. "Imaginary Borges," *New York Review of Books*, XIII (November 20, 1969), 6-10.

Genovés, Antonio. "Algunos aspectos del realismo mágico de Borges," *Cuadernos Hispanoamericanos*, LVI (1963), 571-580.

Gertel, Zunilda A. *Borges y su retorno a la poesía*. Iowa City, University of Iowa Press, and New York, Las Américas, 1967.

———"Jorge Luis Borges y su retorno a la poesía." *Dissertation Abstracts*, XXVIII (1968), 229A (Iowa).

———"La metáfora en la estética de Borges," *Hispania*, LII (1969), 33-39.

Ghiano, Juan Carlos. "Borges, antólogo de sí mismo," *Revista Iberoamericana*, XXIX (1963), 67-87.

———"Borges y la poesía," *Cuadernos Americanos*, XV, Núm. 1 (enero-febrero de 1956), 222-250.

———*Constantes de la literatura argentina*. Buenos Aires, Raigal, 1953. Sobre Borges: págs. 171-172.

———"Destino de Carriego," *Oeste* (Buenos Aires), X, Núm. 17 (1954).

———"Jorge Luis Borges" en su *Poesía argentina del siglo XX* (México-Buenos Aires, Fondo de cultura económica, 1957), págs. 117-124.

———"Lecturas de Borges," *Clima* (Paraná), Núm. 1 (1954).

———Sobre "Nueva refutación del tiempo," *Realidad* (Buenos Aires), IV, Núm. 10 (julio-agosto de 1948), 121.

———"Otras inquisiciones, por J. L. Borges," *Davar* (Buenos Aires), Núm. 42 (septiembre-octubre de 1952), 78-83.

———"Quevedo en las letras argentinas," en su *Temas y actitudes* (Buenos Aires, Ollantay, 1949), págs. 78-79.

Ghida, Arturo. "Discusión sobre Jorge Luis Borges," *Megáfono*, Núm. 11 (agosto de 1933), págs. 19-21.

Ghioldi, Américo. "Un poema civil de Jorge Luis Borges," *El Plata* (Montevideo), 6 de abril de 1954.

Gicovate, Bernardo. Sobre Ana María Barrenechea, *La expresión de la irrealidad en la obra de Jorge Luis Borges, Comparative Literature*, X, Núm. 3 (1958), 270.

Giménez Vega, E. S. "Dos libros, dos hombres," *Histonium* (Buenos Aires), Núm. 146 (enero de 1953).

Giovanni, Norman Thomas di, see di Giovanni, Norman Thomas.

Girondo, Oliverio. *El periódico 'Martín Fierro' (1924-1949)*. Buenos Aires, Colombo, 1949.

Gómez, Carlos Alberto. "Reiteraciones sobre Borges," *Ciudad*, Núms. 2-3 (abril-septiembre de 1955), págs. 32-40.

Gómez Bedate, Pilar. "Sobre Borges," *Cuadernos Hispanoamericanos*, LV (1963), 268-276.

Gómez de la Serna, Ramón. Sobre *El Fervor de Buenos Aires. Revista de Occidente*, IV, Núm. 10 (abril-junio de 1924), 123-127.

Gómez Lance, Betty Rita. "Acerca de Jorge Luis Borges," *La Nueva Democracia* (Nueva York), XXXVIII, Núm. 4 (octubre de 1958), 60-62.

González, César Blas. "Borges y el *Martín Fierro*," *Nexo* (Montevideo), Núm. 1 (abril-mayo de 1955), págs. 56-62.

González, Juan B. Sobre *Inquisiciones*. *Nosotros* (Buenos Aires), XIX, Núm. 193 (junio de 1925), 268-271.

González Casanova, Pablo, "Borges, microcosmos," *Novedades* (México), 23 de marzo de 1951.

González Garaño, Alfredo. "Desagravio a Borges," *Sur*, Núm. 94 (julio de 1942), págs. 14-15.

González Lanuza, Eduardo. "Cinco poetas argentinos," *Sur*, Núm. 98 (1942), págs. 44-74.

————"Desagravio a Borges," *Sur*, Núm. 94 (julio de 1942), págs. 17-18.

————"Jorge Luis Borges, Silvina Ocampo y A. Bioy Casares: *Antología poética argentina*," *Sur*, Núm. 89 (febrero de 1942), págs. 68-69.

————"Marcial Tomayo y Adolfo Ruiz-Díaz: *Borges, enigma y clave*," *Sur*, Núm. 239 (marzo-abril de 1956), págs. 122-124.

Grandov, Oscar V. y Monges, Hebe. "La poesía en Argentina," Universidad nacional del Litoral. Facultad de Filosofía y Letras. Seminario. *Proyección del rosismo en la literatura argentina*. Rosario, Universidad nacional, 1959. Sobre Borges: págs. 66-67.

Grondona, Adela. "¿Por qué escribe usted? contesta Jorge Luis Borges," *Ficción*, Núm. 26 (julio-agosto de 1960), págs. 86-87.

Groussac, Marta Helena. "Carriego, Fernández Moreno y Borges: tres versiones poéticas de Buenos Aires y una línea hacia la poesía vanguardia," *¿Por qué...?*, II, Núm. 15 (s.f.), 6-17.

Grünberg, Carlos M. Sobre *El idioma de los argentinos*. *Vida Literaria* (Buenos Aires), 1929.

Guerra Castellanos, Eduardo. "Un análisis de tiempo y espacio en la producción de Jorge Luis Borges," *Armas y letras*, V, Núms. 1/2 (1962), 56-62.

Guerra, M. A. "Jeroglíficos: A propósito de una composición de Jorge Luis Borges," *Estudios* (Buenos Aires), XXXVIII (1929), 242-245.

Guglielmini, Homero M. Sobre *El Aleph, Clarín* (Buenos Aires), 29 de enero de 1950.

————"Discusión sobre Jorge Luis Borges," *Megáfono*, Núm. 11 (agosto de 1933), págs. 21-22.

Guibert, Rita. "Jorge Luis Borges," *Life en español*, XXI, Núm. 5 (March 11, 1968), 48-60.

Guiraldes, Ricardo. "Una carta inédita," *Síntesis*, II, Núm. 14 (julio de 1928), 155-157.

Gullón, Ricardo. "Borges y su laberinto," *Insula*, XVI, Núm. 175 (1961), 1.

Günther, Helmut. "Jorge Luis Borges," *Welt und Wort* (Tübingen), enero de 1960, pág. 213.

Gunther, John. "A Visit with Argentina's Borges," *Atlantic*, January, 1967, págs. 96-98.

Gutiérrez Girardot, Rafael. "Dos temas en la literatura hispanoamericana," *Cuadernos hispanoamericanos*, Núm. 32 (agosto de 1952), págs. 262-265.

————"Jorge Luis Borges," *Merkur* (Stuttgart), XV, Núm. 155 (1961), 171-178.

————*Jorge Luis Borges: Ensayo de interpretación*. Madrid, *Insula*, 1959.

H

Hamilton, C. D. Sobre *Historia de la eternidad*. *Revista Hispánica Moderna*, XX (1954), 329-330.

Harder, Uffe. "Jorge Luis Borges." in Kristensen, Sven M., ed. *Fremmede digtere i det 20. århundrede.* III (Copenhagen: G.E.C. Grad., 1968), 391-400.

Harss, Luis, y Dohmann, Barbara. "Jorge Luis Borges or the Consolation by Philosophy," en su *Into the Mainstream* (New York, Harper & Row, 1966), págs. 102-136. Edición española: *Los nuestros.* Buenos Aires, Editorial Sudamericana, 1966.

Hart, Thomas R. "The Literary Criticism of Jorge Luis Borges," *Modern Language Notes,* LXXVIII (1963), 489-503.

Heissenbüttel, Helmut. "Parabeln und Legenden," *Neue Deutsche Hefte* (Gütersloh), Núm. 68 (marzo de 1960), págs. 1156-1157.

Henríquez Ureña, Pedro. "Desagravio a Borges," *Sur,* Núm. 94 (julio de 1942), págs. 13-14.

———Sobre *Inquisiciones. Nosotros* (Buenos Aires), XX, Núm. 54 (1926), 138-140.

———Sobre *Inquisiciones. Revista de filología española,* XIII (1926), 79-80.

Hernández Arregui, Juan José. "Jorge Luis Borges y Eduardo Mallea," *Nuestro Tiempo,* V, Núm. 25 (1958), 9-12.

Hoog, Armand. "Au delà de l'énigme: J. L. Borges, *Fictions,*" *Carrefour* (Paris), 26 de marzo, 1952.

"Homenaje a Jorge Luis Borges," *La Voz,* VII (1962), Núm. 2.

Horst, Karl August. "Die Bedeutung des Gaucho bei Jorge Luis Borges," *Merkur* (Stuttgart), Núm. 143 (enero de 1960), págs. 78-84.

———"Nachwort" en Borges, Jorge Luis. *Labyrinthe* (München, C. Hanser, 1959), págs. 291-297.

Ibarra, Néstor. "Jorge Luis Borges en Borges," Jorge Luis *Fictions* (Paris, Gallimard, 1951), págs. 7-13.

———"Jorge Luis Borges," en su *La nueva poesía argentina; ensayo crítico sobre el ultraísmo, 1921-1929* (Buenos Aires, Molinari, 1930), págs. 22-48.

———"Jorge Luis Borges, homme de lettres européen," *Lettres Françaises* (Buenos Aires), Núm. 14 (1944), págs. 9-12.

———"Jorge Luis Borges, poeta," *Síntesis,* III, Núm. 34 (marzo de 1930), 11-32.

Iduarte, Andrés. "Borges es *El Aleph,*" *Revista Hispánica Moderna,* XX, Núms. 1-2 (1954), 75-76.

Irby, James East. "Encuentro con Borges," *Vida Universitaria* (Monterrey), 12 de abril de 1964.

———Murat, Napoleón y Peralta, Carlos. *Encuentro con Borges.* Buenos Aires, Galerna, 1968.

———"Nota sobre *El Aleph* y *El Zahir,*" *Cuadernos del viento* (México), Núm. 3 (octubre de 1960), págs. 39-41.

———"Sobre la estructura de 'Hombre de la esquina Rosada'," *Anuario de Filología* (1962), págs. 157-172.

———"The Structure of the Stories of Jorge Luis Borges," *Dissertation Abstracts,* XXIII, 3377 (Michigan).

J. A. A. "Sobre *El Aleph,*" *Armas y Letras,* I, Núm. 2 (1958), 94-95.

Janssens, Marcel. "Jorge Luis Borges en de bibliotheek van Babel," *Dietsche Warande en Belfort,* CXII (1968), 216-220.

Jarnés, Benjamín. "Sobre *Inquisiciones,*" *Revista de Occidente,* IX, Núm. 25 (1925), 125-127.

I

J

Jitrik, Noé. "*Otras inquisiciones,* Jorge Luis Borges," *Revista Centro* (Buenos Aires), II, Núm. 4 (diciembre de 1952), 35-37.

Jorge Luis Borges. L'Herne, 1964. Michel Maxence, "Avant-Propos: Mériter Borges," págs. 1-3; Rafael Cansinos-Assens, "Evocation de Jorge Luis Borges," pág. 7; "Propos de Mme Leonor Acevedo de Borges," págs. 9-11; Adolfo Bioy Casares, "Lettres et amitiés," págs. 12-18; Victoria Ocampo, "Vision de Jorge Luis Borges," págs. 19-25; Silvina Ocampo, "Images de Borges," págs. 26-30; Emma Risso Platero, "En marchant prés de Borges," págs. 31-32; José Bianco, "Des souvenirs," págs. 33-43; Alicia Jurado, "Borges professeur de littérature," págs. 44-47; César Margrini, "Entrevue avec les élèves de Borges," págs. 48-52; "Correspondance," págs. 53-57: "Jorge Luis Borges à Alfonso Reyes," págs. 55-57; "Textes inédits," págs. 59-100; "Interférences," págs. 101-126; Alfonso Reyes, "L'Argentin Jorge Luis Borges," págs. 103-104; Pierre Drieu la Rochelle, "Borges vaut le voyage," pág. 105; Jean Cassou, "L'exercise problématique de la littérature," págs. 106-108; Maurice Nadeau, "Borges le perturbateur," págs. 109-110; Valéry Larbaud, "Sur Borges," págs. 111-112; Cristina Campo, "La porte magique," págs. 113-114; Michel Bernard, "Le bon usage," págs. 115-116; Ricardo Paseyro, "Ce que gêne ma vue," pág. 117; Anthony Kerrigan, "Borges à Madrid," págs. 118-124; Jean Ricardou, "The God of the Labyrinth," págs. 125-126; Miguel Enguídanos, "Le caractère argentin de Borges," págs. 129-136; Luis Mario Schneider, "La place de Borges dans une histoire du langage argentin," págs. 137-143; André Marcel d'Ans, "Jorge Luis Borges et la poésie d'Amérique," págs. 144-150; Manuel Mujica Lainez, "Borges et les ancêtres," págs. 151-155; Carlos T. de Pereira Lahitte, "Généalogie de Jorge Luis Borges," págs. 156-158; Guillermo de Torre, "Pour la préhistoire ultraïste de Borges," págs. 159-167; Ernesto Sábato, "Les deux Borges," págs. 168-178; Federico Peltzer, "Les-masques de Borges," págs. 179-184; César Magrini, "Fondation mythologique de Borges," págs. 185-193; Roberto Jaurroz, "Adrogué, Borges et les periphéries," págs. 194-195; Nicolas Cocaro, "Borges et les versions du courage," págs. 196-198; Abelardo Castillo, "Borges et la nouvelle génération," págs. 199-204; Rafaël Gutierrez Giradot, "Borges en Allemagne," págs. 205-208; Roger Caillois, "Les thèmes fondamentaux de J. L. Borges," págs. 211-217; Karl August Horst, "Intentions et hasards dans l'œuvre de Borges," págs. 218-223; Maurice-Jean Lefebre, "Qui a écrit Borges," págs. 224-227; Ventura Doreste, "Analyse de Borges," págs. 228-236; Manuel Durán, "Les deux Borges," págs. 237-241; Michel Carrouges, "Borges citoyen de Tlön," págs. 242-244; Rafaël Gutierrez Girardot, "Borges el hacedor," págs. 245-251; Louis Vax, "Borges philosophe," págs. 252-256; Jean Wahl, "Les Personnes et l'impersonnel," págs. 257-264; Rabi, "Fascination de la Kabbale," págs. 265-271; Piétro Citati, "L'imparfait bibliothécaire," págs. 272-275; Claude Ollier, "Thème du texte et du complot," págs. 276-279; Daniel Devoto, "Aleph et Alexis," págs. 280-292; Luis Andrés Murillo, "El inmortal," págs. 293-308; Ana María Barrenechea, "Une fiction de Jorge Luis Borges," págs. 309-311; Marcel Brion, "Masques, miroirs, mensonges et labyrinthe," págs. 312-322; Gérard Genette, "La littérature selon Borges," págs. 323-327; Robert André, "La mort vécue de J. L. Borges," págs. 328-333; André Coyné,

"Une littérature de 'soupçon'," págs. 334-342; Emir Rodríguez Monegal, "Borges essayiste," págs. 343-351; Antonio Regalado, Jr., "Le refus de l'histoire," págs. 352-361; René L. F. Durand, "L'hommage de Borges à *Davar*," págs. 362-364; Paul Bénichou, "Kublai Khan, Coleridge et Borges," págs. 365-368; "Entretiens avec Napoléon Murat," págs. 371-387; "Entretiens avec James E. Irby," págs. 388-403; "Entretiens avec Gloria Alcorta," págs. 404-408; Carlos Peralta, "L'électricité des mots," págs. 408-413; *L'Herne*-Ibarra, "Borges et Borges," págs. 417-465; César Fernández Moreno, "Chronologie de l'ultraïsme," págs. 469-475; Jean de Milleret, "Biographie," págs. 477-479; Juan Montalbán, "Glossaire argentin," págs. 480-484; Nodier Lucio et Lydia Revillo, "Contribution à la bibliographie de Borges," págs. 485-516; "Iconographie," págs. 517-531.

Jurado, Alicia. "Borges y el cuento fantástico," *Ciudad* (Buenos Aires), Núms. 2-3 (abril-septiembre de 1955), págs. 45-49.

————*Genio y figura de Jorge Luis Borges*. Buenos Aires, Editorial Universidad de Buenos Aires, 1964.

Kagel, Jorge. "Días de odio," *Buenos Aires Cine Club,* Núm. 1 (1954).

Kemp, Robert. "La vie des livres. Vérités et Fictions," *Les Nouvelles Littéraires* (Paris), 20 de marzo de 1952.

Kenny, Herbert A. "A Portrait of Jorge Luis Borges," *Globe* (Boston), June 1, 1969, pág. A27.

Kesting, Marianne. "Das hermetische Labyrinth: Zur Dichtung von Jorge Luis Borges," *Neue Deutsche Hefte*, Núm. 107 (1965), págs. 107-124.

Lange, Norah. "Jorge Luis Borges, pensado en algo que no alcanza a ser poema," *Martín Fierro*, 2ª ép., IV, Núm. 40 (28 de abril de 1927), 6.

Lapesa, Rafael. "Borges en Madrid," *Revista de Occidente*, I (1963), 109-112.

Lapouge, Gilles. "Jorge Luis Borges, ce grand homme tout simple," *Figaro Littéraire*, 19-26 de noviembre de 1964.

Lara, Tomás M. "Discusión de Jorge Luis Borges," *Megáfono*, Núm. 11 (agosto de 1933), págs. 22-24.

Laurens, Nélida Gladys. *El cuento en la literatura contemporánea*. Rosario, Edición del autor, 1946.

Leal, Luis. "Los cuentos de Borges," *La Palabra y el Hombre*, II (1963), 417-423.

Léger, Aléxis Saint-Léger. "Carta [de homenaje a Borges]," *Sur*, Núm. 276 (1962), pág. 72.

Lewald, H. Ernest. "The Labyrinth of Time and Place in Two Stories by Borges," *Hispania*, XLV (1962), 630-636.

L'Herne. Véase Jorge Luis Borges.

Lida, Raimundo. "Notas a Borges," *Cuadernos Americanos*, X, Núm. 2 (1951), 286-288.

————"Notas a Borges," *Letras hispánicas: estudios, esquemas* (México-Buenos Aires, Fondo de Cultura económica, 1958), págs. 280-283.

Lima, Robert, "Borges on Borges," en Barrenechea, A. M., *Borges, the Labyrinth Maker* (New York, 1965), págs. 148-153.

————"Jorge Luis Borges. The Labyrinths of Fantasia," *La Voz* (New York), VII, Núm. 2 (1962), 16-17.

————, Corvalan, Octavio, y Braun-Munk, Eugene. "Symposium on Jorge Luis Borges." *La Voz* (New York), VIII, Núm. 8 (1963), 11-13.

K

L

Liscano Velutini, Juan. "Experiencia borgiana," *Revista Nacional de Cultura* (Caracas), XXV (1963), 71-90.

López Palmero, M. Sobre *Cuaderno San Martín*. *Nosotros* (Buenos Aires), XXIV, Núm. 256, tomo 69 (septiembre de 1930), 327-328.

López Ruiz, Juvenal. "Glosa a Jorge Luis Borges," *El Nacional* (Caracas), 20 de marzo de 1958.

Loprete, Carlos Alberto. "Cuentos breves y extraordinarios, por Jorge Luis Borges y Adolfo Bioy Casares," *Ficción* (Buenos Aires), Núm. 3 (septiembre-octubre de 1956), págs. 171-172.

———"*Leopoldo Lugones*, por Jorge Luis Borges," *Ficción* (Buenos Aires), Núm. 2 (julio-agosto de 1956), págs. 172-174.

Lorenz, Erika. "Form und Zeit im Werk des Argentiniers Jorge Luis Borges," *Die Neueren Sprachen*, XVI (1967), 471-484.

Lozada, Salvador María. "Borges y sus detractores," *Ciudad* (Buenos Aires), Núms 2-3 (abril-septiembre de 1955), págs. 40-44.

———"Sobre Borges," *La Gaceta* (Tucumán), 12 de septiembre de 1954.

Lucio, Nodier, y Revello, Lydia. "Contribución a la bibliografía de Jorge Luis Borges," *Bibliografía Argentina de Artes y Letras*, Núms 10-11 (1961), págs. 43-96.

M

Macherey, Pierre. "Borges et le récit fictif," *Temps Modernes*, XXI (1966), 1309-1316.

McKegney, James C. "Buenos Aires in the Poetry of Jorge Luis Borges," *Hispania*, XXVII (1954), 162-166.

Malinow, Ines. "Mensura de la irrealidad en una obra estilística," *La Nación* (Buenos Aires), 27 de abril de 1958.

Malkiel, María Rosa Lida de. "Contribución al estudio de las fuentes literarias de Jorge Luis Borges," *Sur*, Núms. 213-214 (julio-agosto de 1952), págs. 50-57.

———"La visión de trasmundo en las literaturas hispánicas," en Patch, Howard Rollin, *El otro mundo en la literatura medieval*, ed. española (México, Fondo de Cultura Económica, 1956), pág. 449.

Mallea, Eduardo. "Desagravio a Borges," *Sur*, Núm. 94 (julio de 1942), págs. 7-8.

———"Discusión sobre Jorge Luis Borges," *Megáfono*, Núm. 11 (agosto de 1933), págs. 14-16.

———"Un libro de Borges (Apuntes al margen)," *Sagitario* (La Plata), Núm. 6 (1926).

Marechal, Leopoldo. Sobre *Luna de enfrente*. *Martín Fierro*, 2ª ép., II, Núm. 26 (29 de diciembre de 1925), 4.

Marissel, André. "L'univers de Jorge Luis Borges," *Cahiers du Sud*, LI, Núms. 378-379 (1964), 115-124.

Martelli, Juan Carlos. "Ubicación de Jorge Luis Borges," *Ciudad* (Buenos Aires), Núms 2-3 (abril-septiembre de 1955), págs. 50-55.

Marx, Patricia, and John Simon. "Jorge Luis Borges: An Interview." *Commonweal*, LXXXIX (1968), 107-110.

Mastronardi, Carlos. "A vida literária na Argentina," *Journal de Letras* (Rio de Janeiro), Núm. 50 (agosto de 1953).

———"B. Suárez Lynch. Un modelo para la muerte," *Sur*, Núm. 146 (diciembre de 1946), págs. 96-99.

————"Desagravio a Borges," *Sur*, Núm. 94 (julio de 1942), págs. 27-29.

————Sobre *Cuaderno San Martín. Síntesis*, III, Núm. 29 (octubre de 1929), 219-222.

————"Sobre una poesía condenada," *Sur*, Núm. 169 (noviembre de 1948), págs. 52-61.

Maurois, André. "Jorge Luis Borges visto por André Maurois," *Negro sobre blanco* (Buenos Aires), Núm. 20 (1961), págs. 11-12.

Mejía Sánchez, Ernesto. "Biblioteca Americana," *Revista de la Universidad de México*, XV, Núm. 10 (junio de 1961), 29-30.

Méndez, Evar. "Doce poetas nuevos," *Síntesis*, I, Núm. 4 (septiembre de 1927), 15-33.

————"La joven literatura argentina," *El Orden* (Tucumán), 31 de diciembre de 1924.

Merivale, Patricia. "The flaunting of artifice in Vladimir Nabokov and Jorge Luis Borges," in *Nabokov: the Man and his Work*, ed. L. S. Dembo (Madison, University of Wisconsin Press, 1967), págs. 209-229.

Milleret, Jean de. *Entretiens avec J. L. Borges*. Paris, Pierre Belfond, 1967.

Monterroso, Augusto. "Beneficios y maleficios de Jorge Luis Borges," *México en la Cultura* (México), Núm. 636 (22 de mayo de 1961), págs. 2-3.

————"Jorge Luis Borges," *Cultura*, Núm. 7 (1956), págs. 59-62.

————"Jorge Luis Borges," *Novedades* (México), 31 de julio de 1941.

Montgomery, Thomas. "Don Juan Manuel's Tale of Don Illán and Its Revision by Jorge Luis Borges," *Hispania*, XLVII (1964), 464-466.

Morello-Frosch, Martha E. "Elementos populares en la poesía de Jorge Luis Borges," *Asomante*, XVIII, Núm. 3 (1962), 26-35.

Mosquera, Marta. "Borges, el memorioso," *Cuadernos del Congreso por la Libertad de la Cultura*, Núm. 85 (1964), págs. 88-90.

Muñoz, Juan Carlos. "Jorge Luis Borges, juzgado en Suecia," *La Nación* (Buenos Aires), 13 de diciembre de 1964.

Murena, Héctor A. "Condenación de una poesía," *Sur,* Núms. 164-165 (junio-julio de 1948), págs. 76-78.

————*El pecado original de América*. Buenos Aires, Sur, 1954, Sobre Borges: págs. 54-57.

Murillo, L. A. *The Cyclical Night: Irony in James Joyce and Jorge Luis Borges*. Cambridge, Mass., Harvard University Press, 1969.

————"The Labyrinths of Jorge Luis Borges: An Introduction to the Stories of *The Aleph*," *Modern Language Quarterly*, XX, Núm. 3 (1959), 259-266.

Nadeau, Maurice. "Un écrivain déroutant et savoureux: J. L. Borges," *L'Observateur* (Paris), Núm. 94 (28 de febrero de 1952).

Navarro, Joaquina. "Jorge Luis Borges: Taumaturgo de la metáfora," en "Homenaje a Angel del Río," *Revista Hispánica Moderna*, XXXI (1965), 337-344.

Noé, Julio. Sobre *Historia de la eternidad*. *El Hogar* (Buenos Aires), 28 de agosto de 1936, p. 77.

Nuñez, Antonio. "El perfil humano de Jorge Luis Borges," *Insula*, XVIII, Núm. 195 (1963), 5.

Ocampo, Victoria. "Visión de Jorge Luis Borges," *Cuadernos del Congreso por la Libertad de la Cultura,* Núm. 55 (1961), págs. 17-23.

N

O

——"Lettre à Jorge Luis Borges," *Preuves* (Paris), Núm. 162 (1964), págs. 91-92.

——"Saludo a Borges," *Sur*, Núm. 272 (1961), págs. 76-79.

Onís, Federico de. *Antología de la poesía española e hispanoamericana (1882-1932)*. Madrid, Junta para ampliación de estudios e investigaciones científicas. Centro de estudios históricos, 1934. Sobre Borges: págs. 1149-1150.

Orgambide, Pedro G. "Jorge Luis Borges," *Gaceta Literaria* (Buenos Aires), IV, Núm. 20 (mayo de 1960), 23.

Ortelli, Roberto A. "Dos poetas de la nueva generación," *Inicial* (Buenos Aires), I, Núm. 1 (octubre de 1923), 62-68.

Ostrov, Léon. "Discusión sobre Jorge Luis Borges," *Megáfono*, Núm. 11 (agosto de 1933), págs. 24-25.

Pacheco, Armando Correia. "Jorge Luis Borges, escritor universal de América," *Revista Universal* (La Plata), XVI (enero de 1962), 184-188.

——"Simpatías y diferencias," *Revista de la Universidad de México*, XVI (1962), 32.

Pacheco, José Emilio. "Inquisiciones de Borges," *México en la Cultura* (México), Núm. 615 (26 de diciembre de 1960), pág. 4.

——"Las preferencias de un gran escritor," Siempre, Suplemento a *México en la Cultura* (México), Núm. 455 (14 de marzo de 1962), pág. xiv.

——"Los poemas de Borges," *La Gaceta* (México), VI, Núm. 78 (febrero de 1961), 3.

——"Sobre *El hacedor*." *México en la Cultura* (México), Núm. 630 (10 de abril de 1961), pág. 4.

——"36 años en la poesía," *Indice*, XV, Núms 150-151 (julio-agosto de 1961), 7.

Palacio, Ernesto. Sobre *El idioma de los argentinos*. Criterio, I, Núm. 17 (29 de junio de 1928), 533.

Payró, Roberto P. "El mundo literario de Borges," Américas, II, Núm. 10 (octubre de 1950), 37-38.

Peltzer, Federico. "Narrativa argentina contemporánea," *Señales* (Buenos Aires), XII, Núm. 120 (mayo de 1960), 5-10.

Percas, Helena. "Algunas observaciones sobre la lengua de Borges," *Revista Iberoamericana*, XXIII, Núm. 45 (1958), 121-128.

Pereda Valdés, Idelfonso. "Jorge Luis Borges, poeta de Buenos Aires," *Nosotros*, XX, tomo 52 (enero-febrero de 1926), 106-109.

Petit de Murat, Ulises. "Borges as I Know Him, the Writer Who Speaks for Buenos Aires," *Américas*, XI, Núm. 3 (marzo de 1959), 6-11.

——"Discusión sobre Jorge Luis Borges," *Megáfono*, Núm. 11 (agosto de 1933), pág. 14.

——"Jorge Luis Borges y la revolución literaria de *Martín Fierro*," *Correo Literario* (Buenos Aires), 15 de enero de 1944.

Peyrou, Manuel. "Desagravio a Borges," *Sur*, Núm. 94 (julio de 1942), pág. 31.

Pezzoni, Enrique. "Aproximación al último libro de Borges," *Sur*, Núms 217-218 (noviembre-diciembre de 1952), págs. 102-123.

Phillips, Allen W. "El Sur de Borges," *Revista Hispánica Moderna*, XXIX (1963), 140-147.

P

————"Jorge Luis Borges: Leopoldo Lugones," *Nueva Revista de Filología Hispánica*, X, Núms. 3-4 (1956), 449-451.

————"Notas sobre Borges y la crítica reciente," *Revista Iberoamericana*, XXII, Núm. 43 (1957), 41-59.

Pillement, Georges. Sobre *El Fervor de Buenos Aires. Revue de l'Amérique Latine* (Paris), II, Núm. 6 (1923).

Piñer, Virgilio. "Nota sobre la literatura argentina de hoy," *Los Anales de Buenos Aires*, II, Núm. 12 (febrero de 1947), 52-56.

Piñero, Armando Alonso. "The Two Worlds of Jorge Luis Borges," *Américas*, XVII, Núm. 3 (March, 1965), 11-15.

Piñero, Sergio. Sobre *Inquisiciones. Martín Fierro*, 2ª ép., II, Núm. 18 (26 de junio de 1925), 4.

Pinetta, Alberto. "La promesa de la nueva generación literaria," *Síntesis*, III, Núm. 29 (octubre de 1929), 207-218.

Pinto, Joaquín D. "Dos escritores argentinos: *Leopoldo Lugones* por J. L. Borges con la colaboración de B. Edelberg," *La Prensa* (Buenos Aires), 22 de abril de 1956.

Pinto, Juan. *Brevario de literatura argentina contemporánea*. Buenos Aires, La Mandrágora, 1958. Sobre Borges: págs. 97-99 y 216-217.

————"Las calles porteñas en la poesía de Borges," *La Nación* (Buenos Aires), 28 de abril de 1963.

Ponce, Aníbal. "Hojeando los últimos libros," *El Mundo* (Buenos Aires), 15 de julio de 1930.

Prampolini, Santiago. *Historia universal de la literatura*. 2ª ed. española. Buenos Aires, Uteha Argentina, 1955-1958. Sobre Borges, XII, 430-431.

Prieto, Adolfo. "Borges, el ensayo crítico," *Centro* (Buenos Aires), III, Núm. 7 (diciembre de 1953), 9-19.

————*Borges y la nueva generación*. Buenos Aires, Letras Universitarias, 1954.

————"El Martinfierrismo," *Revista de literatura argentina e iberoamericana* (Mendoza), I, Núm. 1 (diciembre de 1959), 9-13.

————"Respuesta de Adolfo Prieto [a la nota de Roy Bartholomew a propósito de *Borges y la nueva generación* de Adolfo Prieto]," *Ciudad* (Buenos Aires), Núms. 2-3 (1955), págs. 101-106.

Quiñones, Fernando. "La argentinidad de Jorge Luis Borges," *La Nación* (Buenos Aires), 12 de abril de 1964.

R. G. P. "Un poema de Borges," *Sur*, Núm. 253 (1958), 69-71.

R. N. "Avez-vous lu Borges?" *Opera* (Paris), Núm. 346 (1952), pág. 3.

Radaelli, Sigrido A. "Discusión sobre Jorge Luis Borges," *Megáfono*, Núm. 11 (agosto de 1933), págs. 29-30.

————"Borges y la memoria de los días," *La Nación* (Buenos Aires), 15 de noviembre de 1964.

Ramela, Carlos. "Influencia e imitación de Jorge Luis Borges," *Marcha* (Montevideo), 8 de octubre de 1948.

————"Escritura y enigmas de Jorge Luis Borges," *Marcha* (Montevideo), 23 de junio de 1950.

Ramos, Abelardo. *Crisis y resurrección de la literatura argentina*. Apéndice: *Polémica Sábato-Ramos*. Buenos Aires, Coyoacán, 1961.

Q

R

Rangel Guerra, Alfonso. "La realidad en algunos cuentos de Borges," *Vida Universitaria* (Monterrey), 12 de abril de 1954.

Real de Azúa, Carlos, Rama, Angel, and Rodríguez Monegal, Emir. *Evasión y arraigo de Borges y Neruda*. Montevideo, Tall. Gráf. Ligu, 1960.

Réda, Jacques. "Commentaire de l'*Immortel* de Jorge Luis Borges," *Cahiers du Sud*, XLIX, Núm. 370 (1962), 435-455.

———"L'Herne: *Jorge Borges*," *Cahiers du Sud*, LI, Núms. 378-379 (1964), 155-157.

Rega Molina, Horacio. Sobre "El compadrito," *El Mundo* (Buenos Aires), 18 de junio de 1945.

Rest, Jaime. "Borges, Descartes y el obispo Wilkins," *Centro* (Buenos Aires), II, Núm. 4 (diciembre de 1952), 47-48.

Revista de Occidente, Madrid. *Diccionario de literatura española*. 2ª ed. Madrid, Revista de Occidente, 1953. Sobre Borges: pág. 98.

Revol, Enrique Luis. "Aproximación a la obra de Jorge Luis Borges," *Cuadernos del Congreso por la Libertad de la Cultura* (Paris), Núm. 5 (1954), págs. 20-28.

———"Jorge Luis Borges," *Belfagor* (Messina-Firenze), IV, Núm. 4 (julio de 1949), 425-430.

Reyes, Alfonso. "El argentino Jorge Luis Borges," en su *Los trabajos y los días (1934-1944)*. (México, 1945), págs. 133-135.

———"El argentino Jorge Luis Borges," en su *Obras Completas*, IX (México, 1959), págs. 307-309.

———"Misterio en la Argentina," *Tiempo* (México), 30 de julio de 1943.

———*El deslinde. Prolegómenos a la teoría literaria*. México, El Colegio de México, 1944. Sobre Borges, págs. 14n, 50n, 110, 122, 203 y 307.

Reyes, Salvador. Sobre *El fervor de Buenos Aires*. Zig-Zag (Santiago de Chile), XIX, Núm. 972 (octubre de 1923).

Ríos Patrón, José Luis. "Bibliografía de Jorge Luis Borges," *Ciudad* (Buenos Aires), Núms 2-3 (1955), págs. 56-62.

———"El laberinto de Borges," *Sur*, Núm. 233 (marzo-abril de 1955), págs. 75-79.

———*Jorge Luis Borges*. Buenos Aires, La Mandrágora, 1955.

———"Sobre un cuento de Borges," *Zohra* (Buenos Aires), Núm. 7 (1955).

———. con el seud. Horacio Jorge Becco. "Vicente Rossi y Jorge Luis Borges," en Rossi, Vicente. *Cosas de negros* (Buenos Aires, Hachette, 1958), págs. 22-25.

Rivero Olazábal, Raúl. "Discusión sobre Jorge Luis Borges," *Megáfono*, Núm. 11 (agosto de 1933), págs. 17-18.

Rodríguez Monegal, Emir. *Borges*. Paris, Editions du Seuil, 1969.

———"Borges como crítico literario," *La Palabra y el Hombre* (Veracruz), Núm. 31 (julio-agosto de 1964), 411-416.

———"Borges, el memorioso," *Marcha* (Montevideo), Núm. 618 (1952).

———"Borges, entre Escila y Caribdis," en *El juicio de los parricidas; la nueva generación argentina y sus maestros* (Buenos Aires, Deucalión, 1956), págs. 55-79.

———"Borges: teoría y práctica," *Número* (Montevideo), VI, Núm. 27 (diciembre de 1955), 124-157.

———"Con Borges en Buenos Aires," *Revista Mexicana Literatura*, Núms. 5/6 (1964), págs. 12-22.

————"El último avatar borgiano," *Marcha* (Montevideo), 8 de junio de 1956.

————"Jorge Luis Borges," en *Lexicon der Weltliteratur im 20. Jahrhundert* (Freiburg, Herder, 1960), I, 226-228.

————"Jorge Luis Borges," *Marcha* (Montevideo), 12 de septiembre de 1953.

————"Jorge Luis Borges y la literatura fantástica," en su *Narradores de esta América* (Montevideo, Alfa, s.f.), págs. 81-96.

————"Macedonio Fernández, Borges y el ultraísmo," *Número* (Montevideo), IV, Núm. 19 (abril-junio de 1952), 171-183.

Roggiano, Alfredo Angel. "Borges, Jorge Luis," en *Diccionario de la literatura latinoamericana* (Washington, Unión Panamericana, 1961), II, 253-258.

Romero, Francisco. "Desagravio a Borges," *Sur*, Núm. 94 (julio de 1942), pág. 9.

Rose, Gonzalo. "Itinerario del tiempo en la ciudad de Borges," *Novedades* (México), 6 de diciembre de 1953.

Rosenblat, Angel. "Desagravio a Borges," *Sur*, Núm. 94 (julio de 1942), pág. 23.

Rubens, Erwin F. "Discusión sobre Jorge Luis Borges," *Megáfono*, Núm. 11 (agosto de 1933), págs. 30-33.

Ruiz, Luis Alberto. *Diccionario de la literatura universal*. Buenos Aires. Raigal, 1955-1956. Sobre Borges: I, 200.

Ruiz-Díaz, Adolfo. "Borges en su 'arte poética'," *Revista de Literaturas Modernas* (Mendoza), Núm. 6 (1967), págs. 11-25.

————Véase también Tamayo, Marcial.

Rumazo, Lupe. "Intento de exégesis de Jorge Luis Borges," *El Universal* (Caracas), 17 de noviembre de 1964.

Running, Thorpe. "The Problem of Time in the Work of Jorge Luis Borges," *Discourse*, IX (1966), 296-308.

S. P. M. "Jorge Luis Borges en francés," *La Nación* (Buenos Aires), 22 de enero de 1953.

Sábato, Ernesto. "Borges y Borges," *Revista de la Universidad de México*, XVIII (1964), 22-26.

————"Borges y Borges, el argentino y la metafísica," *Vida Universitaria* (Monterrey), 12 de abril de 1964.

————"Desagravio a Borges," *Sur*, Núm. 94 (julio de 1942), págs. 30-31.

————"En torno de Borges," *Casa de las Américas*, III, Núms. 17-18 (1963), 7-12.

————*Heterodoxia*. Buenos Aires, Emecé, 1953.

————"Los dos Borges," *Indice*, XV, Núms. 150-151 (julio-agosto de 1961), 6-7.

————"Los relatos de Jorge Luis Borges," *Sur*, Núm. 125 (febrero de 1945), págs. 69-75.

————"Sobre el método histórico de Jorge Luis Borges," *Ficción* (Buenos Aires), Núm. 7 (mayo-junio de 1957), págs. 86-89.

————*Tres aproximaciones a la literatura de nuestro tiempo: Robbe-Grillet, Borges, Sartre*. Santiago de Chile, Editorial Universitaria, 1968.

————"Una efusión de Jorge Luis Borges," *Ficción* (Buenos Aires), Núm. 4 (noviembre-diciembre de 1956), págs. 80-82.

————*Uno y el universo*. Buenos Aires, Sudamericana, 1945. Sobre Borges: págs. 21-27, 104-108.

Saint-Phalle, Thérèse de. "Jorge Luis Borges, le plus grand écrivain argentin, croit que ses livres ne valent rien," *Figaro Littéraire*, 16 de febrero de 1963.

Sainz de Robles, Federico Carlos. *Ensayo de un diccionario de la literatura.*

S

Madrid, Aguilar, 1949-1950. Sobre Borges: II, 204-205. 2a ed., 1953-1956, II, 151-152.

Sánchez, Luis Alberto. "Jorge Luis Borges," *La Nueva Democracia*, XLII, Núm. 4 (1962), 44-52.

————*Proceso y contenido de la novela hispanoamericana.* Madrid, Gredos, 1953. Sobre Borges: pág. 468.

Sánchez Reulet, Aníbal. "Desagravio a Borges," *Sur*, Núm. 94 (julio de 1942), pág. 19.

Sánchez Riva, Arturo. "Sobre novelas policiales," *Sur*, Núm. 143 (septiembre de 1946), págs. 69-73.

Santana, Lázaro. "La vida y la brújula." (Conversación con Borges) *Insula*, XXIII, Núm. 258 (mayo de 1968), 1, 4-5.

Scholes, Robert. "A commentary on 'The theme of the traitor and the hero'," in *Elements of Fiction* (London, Oxford University Press, 1968), págs. 83-88.

Siebenmann, Gustav. "Jorge Luis Borges: Ein neuer Typus des lateinamerikanischen Schriftstellers." *Germanisch-Romanische Monatsschrift*, Neue Folge, XVI (1966), 297-314.

Simms, Ruth L. Conzelman. "Un vistazo a la poesía de Jorge Luis Borges," *Hispania*, XXXV (1952), 414-418.

Solero, F. J. "Borges, o el estilo como acecho de la realidad," *La Nación* (Buenos Aires), 23 de diciembre de 1951.

Soria, H. "Borges y su obsesión del compadrito," *Gaceta Literaria* (Buenos Aires), I, Núm. 1 (febrero de 1956), 16.

Sosa López, Emilio. "Tendencias de la poesía argentina actual," *Realidad* (Buenos Aires), V, Núm. 13 (1949), 73-80.

Soto, Luis Emilio. "Desagravio a Borges," *Sur*, Núm. 94 (julio de 1942), págs. 9-12.

————"El cuento," en Arrieta, Rafael Alberto, dir. *Historia de la literatura argentina* (Buenos Aires, Peuser, 1958-1960), IV, 285-450. Sobre Borges: págs. 398-400.

————"El sentido poético de la ciudad moderna," *Proa*, 2ª ép., I, Núm. 1 (agosto de 1924), 11-20.

Sotomayor, Miguel. "El Aleph," *Criterio* (Buenos Aires), XXIII, Núm. 1112 (23 de marzo de 1950), 199-200.

Speratti Piñero, Emma Susana. *Jorge Luis Borges.* San Luis Potosí, Inst. Potosino de Bellas Artes, 1959.

Spivakovsky, Erika. "In Search of Arabic Influences on Borges." *Hispania*, LI (1968), 223-231.

Starosviezky, S. "Borges, nada más que un sueño argentino," *Revista del Centro Estudiantes de Periodismo*, Núm. 2 (diciembre de 1957), pág. 7.

Stéfano, Rafael. "Crítica de una crisis," *Gaceta Literaria* (Buenos Aires), III, Núm. 19 (1959), 3-4 y 6.

Stevens, Harriet S. "Infiernos de Borges," *Insula*, XVIII, Núm. 194 (1963), 1, 13.

Sucre, Guillermo. *Borges, el poeta.* México, Universidad Nacional autónoma, 1967. 2ª ed. Caracas, Monte Avila, 1968.

Talese, Gay. "Argentine Here on Tour Finds Advantage in Blindness," *New York Times*, February 5, 1962.

T

Tamayo, Marcial and Ruiz-Díaz, Adolfo. *Borges, enigma y clave*. Buenos Aires, *Nuestro Tiempo*, 1955.

Tello, Jaime. "Jorge Luis Borges," *Bolívar* (Bogotá), Núm. 7 (1952), pág. 411-414.

Tentori Montalto, Francesco. "Prefazione [a *L'Aleph*]," en Borges, Jorge Luis, *L'Aleph* (Milano, Feltrinelli, 1959), págs. 9-16.

Tiempo, César, y Vignale, Pedro-Juan. *Exposición de la actual poesía argentina*. Buenos Aires, 1927.

Times (London) *Literary Supplement*. "Poetry from Latin America," May 22, 1948.

Tomat-Guido, Francisco. "*El hacedor*, por Jorge Luis Borges," *Davar* (Buenos Aires), Núm. 89 (abril-junio de 1961), págs. 119-120.

Toppani, Gabriela. "Intervista con Borges," *Verri*, VIII (1964), 97-105.

Torre, Guillermo de. *Literaturas europeas de vanguardia*. Madrid, Raggio, 1925. Sobre Borges: págs. 62-65.

————"Márgenes de ultraísmo. Esquemas para una liquidación de valores," *Proa*, II, Núm. 10 (s.f.), 21-29.

————"Para la prehistoria ultraísta de Borges," *Hispania*, XLVII (1964), 457-463.

————"Para la prehistoria ultraísta de Borges," *Cuadernos Hispanoamericanos*, LVII (1964), 5-15.

————Sobre *Luna de enfrente*. *Revista de Occidente*, XI, Núm. 33 (enero-marzo de 1926), 409-411.

Torres-Rioseco, Arturo. *Nueva historia de la gran literatura iberoamericana*. 3ª ed. Buenos Aires, Emecé, 1960. Sobre Borges: págs. 271-272.

Tyre, Carl S. "Jorge Luis Borges," *Hispania*, XLV (1962), 80-82.

Ulloa, M. E. "Borges, conferenciante," *Sur*, Núms. 213-214 (julio-agosto de 1952), pág. 168.

Updike, John. "The Author as Librarian," *The New Yorker*, October 30, 1965, 223-246.

Van Praag-Chantraine, Jacqueline. "Jorge Luis Borges ou la mort au bout du labyrinthe," *Synthèses*, Núm. 236-237 (enero-febrero de 1966), págs. 117-126.

Vásquez, María Esther. "Everness: an approach to the poetry of Jorge Luis Borges," trans. Ronald Christ and Paschal Cantatore. *Tri Quarterly*, XV (1969), 245-257.

Vax, Louis. *L'art et littérature fantastiques*. Paris, Presses Universitaires de France, 1960. Sobre Borges: págs. 115-118.

Verbitsky, Bernardo. "Un libro de Jorge Luis Borges," *Noticias Gráficas* (Buenos Aires), 5 de mayo de 1942.

Verdevoye, Paul. "*Ficciones* de Jorge Luis Borges y *Fictions* de Paul Verdevoye," *Buenos Aires Literaria*, Núm. 11 (agosto de 1953), págs. 39-43.

Videla, Gloria. "Poemas y prosas olvidados de Borges," *Revista de Literatura Argentina e Iberoamericana*, III, Núm. 3 (1961), 101-105.

Vignale, Pedro Juan. "Discusión sobre Luis Borges," *Megáfono*, Núm. 11 (agosto de 1933), págs. 27-28.

Villaurrutia, Xavier. Sobre *Poemas*. *El hijo pródigo* (México), IV (1944), 61.

U

V

————Sobre *Ficciones*. *El hijo pródigo* (México), VIII (1945), 119.

Virasoro, Miguel A. Sobre *El idioma de los argentinos*. *Síntesis*, II, Núm. 14 (julio de 1928), 265-267.

Viry, Amé de. "Borges ou l'élément romanesque," *Nouvelle Revue Française*, XIII (1965), 1069-1079.

Vitier, Cintio. "En torno a la poesía de J. L. Borges," *Orígenes* (La Habana), II, Núm. 6 (julio de 1945), 33-42.

W

Wais, Kurt. "Anatomie der Melancholie—Über Jorge Luis Borges," *Institut für Auslandsbeziehungen*, Mitteilungen (Stuttgart), Núms. 2-3 (abril-septiembre, 1961), págs. 131-135.

Weber, Frances W. "Borges' Stories: Fiction and Philosophy." *Hispanic Review*, XXXVI (1968), 124-141.

Weiss, Alfredo J. "Borges traducido al francés," *Sur*, Núms 213-214 (julio-agosto de 1952), págs. 165-166.

————Sobre *El Aleph*. *Reunión* (Buenos Aires), I, Núm. 4 (1949).

Wheelock, Kinch Carter. "The Mythmaker: A Study of Motif and Symbol in the Short Stories of Jorge Luis Borges," *Dissertation Abstracts*, XXVII (1966), 489A (Texas).

Wilk, Werner. "Magisches aus Buenos Aires," *Die Bücher-Kommentare*, 1º trimestre de 1960.

Wolberg, Issac. *Jorge Luis Borges*. Buenos Aires, Ediciones Culturales Argentinas, 1961.

X

Xirau, Ramón. "Borges o el elogio de la sensibilidad," *La Palabra y el Hombre* (Xalapa), Núm. 14 (1960), págs. 81-89.

————"Borges y las refutaciones del tiempo," *Revista Mexicana Literatura*, Núms. 5/6 (1964), págs. 5-11.

Y

Yates, Donald A. "Borges y la literatura fantástica," *Kentucky Foreign Language Quarterly*, XIII (1967), 34-40.

Yunque, Alvaro seud. de Arístides Gandolfi Herrero. "*El idioma*, por Jorge Luis Borges y Jorá Edmundo Clemente," *Davar* (Buenos Aires), Núm. 48 (septiembre-octubre de 1953), págs. 95-97.

Z

Zía, Lisardo. "Discusión sobre Jorge Luis Borges," *Megáfono*, Núm. 11 (agosto de 1933), págs. 25-27.

Zum Felde, Alberto. *Indice crítico de la literatura hispanoamericana*. México, Guaranía, 1954-1959. Sobre Borges: I, 563-584, II, 451-456.

Addendum

C. M. M., *Marcha* (Montevideo), 9-7-1948.

Comentario (Buenos Aires), abril-junio de 1954.

El Diario (Paraná), 9-2-1947.

Latitud (Buenos Aires), I, Núm. 1 (1953). Sobre *Contestación a una encuesta*.

Latitud (Buenos Aires), XXXIV, 15-12-1949.

La Libertad (España), 6-10-1929.

Marcha (Montevideo), 28-7-1959. Sobre *Otra imagen de James*.

La Nación (Buenos Aires), 26-9-1954.
El Plata (Montevideo), 2-9-1947.
El Plata (Montevideo), 2-9-1949.
Valeurs (Paris), X, julio de 1945.
Ocampo, Victoria. *Diálogo con Borges.* Buenos Aires, Sur, 1969.

Jorge Luis Borges:

Selected Bibliography of First Editions and English Translations

By THOMAS E. LYON

L ike that of most great authors, the bibliography of Jorge Luis Borges presents numerous difficulties. One obvious problem is the republication of the same volume with the addition of several new creations, witness the frequent editions of *Poemas* and *Obra poética* each with a few new titles. The present bibliography embodies only first editions and important innovative reeditions essential for a comprehension of Borges' literary trajectory. In recent years Borges has published considerable creative work in collaboration with several Argentine writers and this prose is included as part of the bibliography. Finally a list of English translations is added for North American students.

University of Wisconsin

Poetry

Fervor de Buenos Aires. Buenos Aires, Imprenta Serantes, 1923.
Luna de enfrente. Buenos Aires, Proa, 1925.
Cuaderno San Martín. Buenos Aires, Proa, 1929.
Poemas, 1922-1943. Buenos Aires, Losada, 1943.
Poemas, 1923-1953. Buenos Aires, Emecé, 1954.
Poemas, 1923-1958. Buenos Aires, Emecé, 1958.
El hacedor. Buenos Aires, Emecé, 1960. Combination of prose and poetry.
Antología personal. Buenos Aires, Sur, 1961. Prose and poetry.
Obra poética, 1923-1964. Buenos Aires, Emecé, 1964.
Para las seis cuerdas. Buenos Aires, Emecé, 1965.
Obra poética, 1923-1967. Buenos Aires, Emecé, 1967.
Nueva antología personal. Buenos Aires, Emecé, 1968. Prose and poetry.

Obra poética de Borges:
  I. *Fervor de Buenos Aires, 1923*. Buenos Aires, Emecé, 1969. Revised edition.
 II. *Luna de enfrente / Cuaderno San Martín, 1925-1929*. Buenos Aires, Emecé, 1969. Revised edition.

III. *El otro, el mismo, 1930-1967.* Buenos Aires, Emecé, 1969.
IV. *Elogio de la sombra, 1967-1969.* Buenos Aires, Emecé, 1969. Prose and
    poetry.

Fiction

Historia universal de la infamia. Buenos Aires, Tor, 1935. 1954 edition has some
    new pieces added.
El jardín de los senderos que se bifurcan. Buenos Aires, Sur, 1941.
Ficciones. Buenos Aires, Sur, 1944. 1956 edition has some new additions.
El Aleph. Buenos Aires, Losada, 1949. Some additions and changes in the 1952
    and 1957 editions.
La muerte y la brújula, Buenos Aires, Emecé, 1951.
El informe de Brodie. Buenos Aires, Emecé, 1970.
Prose pieces in *El hacedor, Antología personal, Nueva antología personal,* and
    Elogio de la sombra, already documented in the section on poetry.

Essay

Inquisiciones. Buenos Aires, Proa, 1925.
El tamaño de mi esperanza. Buenos Aires, Proa, 1926.
El idioma de los argentinos. Buenos Aires, M. Gleizer, 1928.
Evaristo Carriego. Buenos Aires, M. Gleizer, 1930.
Discusión. Buenos Aires, M. Gleizer, 1932.
Las Kenningar. Buenos Aires, Colombo, 1933.
Historia de la eternidad. Buenos Aires, Viau y Zona, 1936.
Nueva refutación del tiempo. Buenos Aires, Oportet y Haereses, 1947.
Aspectos de la literatura gauchesca. Montevideo, Número, 1950.
Otras inquisiciones, 1937-1952. Buenos Aires, Sur, 1952.
La poesía gauchesca. Buenos Aires, Centro de Estudios Brasileiros, 1960.
Macedonio Fernández. Buenos Aires, Ediciones Culturales Argentinas, 1961.

Works Done In Collaboration

J.L.B. and Adolfo Bioy Casares (often with the pseudonym of H. Bustos
    Domecq):
Seis problemas para don Isidro Parodi. Buenos Aires, Sur, 1942.
Dos fantasías memorables. Buenos Aires, Oportet y Haereses, 1946.
Un modelo para la muerte. Buenos Aires, Oportet y Haereses, 1946.
Los orilleros. El paraíso de los creyentes. Buenos Aires, Losada, 1955. Two movie
    scripts.
Crónicas de Bustos Domecq. Buenos Aires, Emecé, 1967.

J.L.B. and Betina Edelberg. *Leopoldo Lugones.* Buenos Aires, Troquel, 1955.

J.L.B. and Margarita Guerrero:

El Martín Fierro. Buenos Aires, Columba, 1953.
Manual de zoología fantástica. México, Fondo de Cultura Económica, 1957.

El libro de seres imaginarios. Buenos Aires, Kier, 1967.

J.L.B. and Luisa Mercedes Levinson. *La hermana de Eloísa.* Buenos Aires, Ene, 1955.

English Translations

Labyrinths. Selected Stories and Other Writings. New York, New Directions, 1962. Edited by Donald Yates and James Irby.

Ficciones. New York, Grove Press, 1962. Edited by Anthony Kerrigan.

Dreamtigers. Austin, University of Texas Press, 1964. Translators Mildred Boyer and Harold Morland. Translation of *El hacedor.*

Other Inquisitions, 1937-1952. Austin, University of Texas Press, 1964. Translator Ruth L. Simms.

A Personal Anthology. New York, Grove Press, 1967. Edited by Anthony Kerrigan.

The Book of Imaginary Beings. New York, Dutton, 1969. Translated by Norman Thomas di Giovanni in collaboration with the author.

The Aleph and Other Stories. New York, Dutton, 1970. Translated by Norman Thomas di Giovanni in collaboration with the author.

Jorge Luis Borges

in *Books Abroad* (1936-1971)

1. *Historia universal de la infamia* (Buenos Aires. Tor. 1935), reviewed by Samuel Putnam in *BA* 10:4, pp. 470-471.

2. *Ficciones* (Buenos Aires. Sur. 1944), reviewed by Roy Temple House in *BA* 20:1, pp. 53-54.

3. *La muerte y la brújula* (Buenos Aires. Emecé. 1951), reviewed by Richard Armitage in *BA* 27:3, p. 265.

4. *Otras inquisiciones* (Buenos Aires. Sur. 1952), reviewed by José Antonio Portuondo in *BA* 29:4, pp. 414-415.

5. *Poemas 1923-1953* (Buenos Aires. Emecé. 1954), reviewed by Kathleen Chase in *BA* 30:1, p. 37.

6. *Poesía gauchesca*, 2 vols. (Mexico. Fondo de Cultura Económica. 1955), reviewed by Edward Larocque Tinker in *BA* 30:1, p. 72.

7. *Historia de la eternidad. Historia universal de la infamia*, 2 vols. (Buenos Aires. Emecé. 1953, 1954), reviewed by Kathleen Chase in *BA* 30:4, p. 400.

8. In coll. with Adolfo Bioy Casares. *Los orilleros. El paraíso de los creyentes* (Buenos Aires. Losada. 1955), reviewed by Willis Knapp Jones in *BA* 32:1, p. 69.

9. In coll. with Marguerita Guerrero. *Manual de zoología fantástica* (México. Fondo de Cultura Económica. 1957), reviewed by David Sanders in *BA* 32:2, p. 174.

10. *Antología personal* (Buenos Aires. Sur. 1961), reviewed by H. Ernest Lewald in *BA* 36:3, p. 300.

11. *Ficciones*. Anthony Kerrigan, ed. (New York. Grove. 1962), reviewed by Bernice G. Duncan in *BA* 37:3, p. 338.

12. *Labyrinths: Selected Stories and Other Writings*. Donald A. Yates, James E. Irby, eds. (New York. New Directions. 1962), reviewed by Bernice G. Duncan in *BA* 37:3, p. 338.

13. In coll. with María Esther Vázquez. *Introducción a la literatura inglesa* (Buenos Aires. Columbia. 1965), reviewed by Bernice G. Duncan in *BA* 40:4, p. 453.

14. In coll. with Adolfo Bioy Casares. *Cuentos breves y extraordinarios* (Buenos Aires. Santiago Rueda. 1967), reviewed by R. Ardila in *BA* 43:2, p. 239.

15. Donald A. Yates, "Borges in Books" in *BA* 44:1, pp. 17-22.

16. Carter Wheelock. *The Mythmaker: A Study of Motif and Symbol in the Short Stories of Jorge Luis Borges* (Austin, Texas. University of Texas Press. 1969), reviewed by David W. Foster in *BA* 44:3, p. 452.

17. Ronald Christ. *The Narrow Act. Borges' Art of Allusion* (New York. New York University Press. 1969), reviewed by Marta Morello-Frosch in *BA* 44:4, pp. 638-639.

18. Ibarra. *Borges et Borges* (Paris. L'Herne. 1969), reviewed by Henry Kahane in *BA* 45:1, pp. 91-92.

19. H. Ernest Lewald, "Argentine Literature: National or European?" in *BA* 45:2, pp. 217-225.

20. Martin S. Stabb. *Jorge Luis Borges* (New York. Twayne. 1970), reviewed by Emir Rodríguez Monegal in *BA* 45:2, pp. 294-295.

21. *The Aleph and Other Stories.* Norman Thomas di Giovanni, ed. & tr. (New York. Dutton. 1970), reviewed by Thomas E. Lyon in *BA* 45:3, pp. 496-497.

22. *El informe de Brodie* (Buenos Aires. Emecé. 1970), reviewed by Donald A. Yates in *BA* 45:3, p. 486.

Notes on Contributors

Jaime Alazraki is Associate Professor of Spanish in the University of California at San Diego, La Jolla.

Ronald Christ is Assistant Professor of English at Livingston College, Rutgers University in New Brunswick, New Jersey.

Lowell Dunham is Professor and Chairman of the Department of Modern Languages in the University of Oklahoma, Norman.

Robert L. Fiore is Assistant Professor of Romance Languages in Michigan State University, East Lansing.

Norman Thomas di Giovanni is one of the principal English translators of Borges. He has edited *Cántico: A Selection* by Jorge Guillén and lives in Buenos Aires.

Jorge Guillén is a celebrated Castilian poet, author of *Cántico, Clamor, Homenaje*. He often resides in Cambridge, Massachusetts.

James East Irby is Associate Professor of Spanish in Princeton University.

Ivar Ivask is an Estonian poet, Professor of Modern Languages, and editor of the international literary quarterly *Books Abroad* in the University of Oklahoma, Norman.

Thomas E. Lyon is Assistant Professor of Spanish in the University of Wisconsin, Madison.

John Cameron Murchison is Instructor of Romance Languages at Tufts University in Medford, Massachusetts.

Emir Rodríguez Monegal is Professor of Spanish and Chairman of Latin American Studies in Yale University.

Donald A. Yates is Professor of Spanish in Michigan State University, East Lansing.

113